God of Earth

For Allison
Love, Hampton

God of Earth

Discovering a Radically Ecological Christianity

Kristin Swenson

(Slingluff)

WJK WESTMINSTER
JOHN KNOX PRESS
LOUISVILLE · KENTUCKY

First edition
Published by Westminster John Knox Press
Louisville, Kentucky

16 17 18 19 20 21 22 23 24 25—10 9 8 7 6 5 4 3 2 1

Book design by Drew Stevens
Cover design by Allison Taylor

Library of Congress Cataloging-in-Publication Data

Names: Swenson, Kristin M., author.
Title: God of earth : discovering a radically ecological christianity / Kristin Swenson.
Description: First edition. | Louisville, KY : Westminster John Knox Press, 2016.
Identifiers: LCCN 2016013580 (print) | LCCN 2016024265 (ebook) | ISBN 9780664261573 (pbk. : alk. paper) | ISBN 9781611647563 (ebk.)
Subjects: LCSH: God (Christianity)--Omnipresence. | Incarnation. | Jesus Christ. | Creation.
Classification: LCC BT132 .S94 2016 (print) | LCC BT132 (ebook) | DDC 231.7—dc23
LC record available at https://lccn.loc.gov/2016013580

Most Westminster John Knox Press books are available at special quantity discounts when purchased in bulk by corporations, organizations, and special-interest groups. For more information, please e-mail SpecialSales@wjkbooks.com.

For Craig

Contents

Acknowledgments

Slight as it is, this book has been a long time coming. After all, it reflects thoughts and ideas inspired, encouraged, and informed by innumerable conversations and the work of countless others. Many people have lent all kinds of assistance along the way—more people, I regret to say, than I'm remembering to list here.

I wish to thank especially Gigi Amateau, Bethany Carlson, Cliff Edwards, Stephanie Pearson, Larry and Nyla Rasmussen, Vera Katelyn Sack, Lisa Russ Spaar, and Anne Westrick. I'm grateful to my group of Richmond women writers, and to those in Charlottesville, too. A coincidence of courses at St. Olaf College many years ago taught by Eugene Bakko, Vern Faillettaz, and Gary Stansell ignited some of what's articulated here. And to oh, the many wonderful human beings who have toiled to write about environmental issues, spirituality, beauty, faith, nature, God . . . and from every conceivable genre, thank you, thank you, thank you.

Thanks also to my agent Joanne Wyckoff and to the folks at Westminster John Knox Press, especially Jessica Miller Kelley, Julie Tonini, Alison Wingfield, and Stacie Kizer for taking this on. I'm grateful for permissions granted from Copper Canyon Press and poet Chase Twichell; Farrar, Straus, and Giroux and poet Charles Wright; Susan Gilbert for the Sydney Carter lyrics; Peter Mayer; and Kathleen Dean Moore.

Thanks to Mom and Dad, always. And to my husband, Craig Slingluff, without whom this project would have languished as a muddle of half bits scattered around my office and brain until the latter was no more, thank you. I have dedicated this book to him.

Introduction

"The temple bell stops.
But the sound keeps coming
out of the flowers."

—Basho, translated by Robert Bly

One of the enduring wonders of writing is how often what shows up on the page surprises me, the writer of it, as much as (maybe more than) any reader. Sometimes as I hunker there, laying down the text, word by word, brick by brick, I bang smack into something I didn't even know existed before. A glimmering idea, brand new, floats down and lands all shiny in the mortar. Suddenly, while writing what I supposedly know, I stumble upon a beauty or a truth that I'd never even suspected before. Grace of the muses, the ancient Greeks might say.

I did not expect, in working on this project, to happen upon a comfort that has eluded me for as long as I can remember. I'd begun to think I would never find equanimity in the face of our planet's ills. Wonder of wonders, this project gave me a sudden and profound (if fleeting) relief that requires neither that I fix everything, nor that I pretend there's no problem and preoccupy myself with the bread and circus of business as usual. It's admittedly a slippery peace—just as (but only as) slippery as faith, I suppose.

A lapsed churchgoer of a questionable Christianity, I nevertheless remain captivated by the implications of Jesus. I cannot shake the sense that the premise at the heart of Christianity is rich in ways as yet unplumbed and profoundly relevant for our time. I look around at the world as it is, *caring* about the world as it is, and wonder if the Jesus of Christian theology just might be bigger than the Middle Eastern man from two thousand years ago.

I was born, raised, and still identify myself as a Christian; and for as long as I can remember, I've been passionate about the health and welfare of the nonhuman natural world. Over the years, both general characteristics—my Christianity and environmentalism—have taken on all sorts of nuance, from embarrassment over what frequently stands for "Christian" and attendant religion envy (Buddhism is so cool, and Jewish ritual rocks), to appreciating how sophisticated our interactions with the nonhuman natural world must be in order to do the least harm.

I've come to agree with Jane Goodall, who said, "How sad that so many people seem to think that science and religion are mutually exclusive."[1] And with Wendell Berry that "perhaps the great disaster of human history is one that happened to or within religion: that is, the conceptual division between the holy and the world, the excerpting of the Creator from the creation."[2] So to state this project in another way: I see hints of ways within the religion I inherited to put things together again—the holy and the world, Creator and creation.

What if Jesus, the incarnation of a universal and eternal God who desires reconciliation and fullness of life, is also present and alive with us today, in and through this pulsing blue-green planet Earth? What does it mean for the ever-living God of all to become flesh that we might be reconciled to her? What if among the ways that a person might meet the incarnate God, know divine love, and experience deepest forgiveness is in relationship to the nonhuman natural world?

I propose taking Christian claims seriously—but in a new way, to come at it all quite differently. What if Jesus, from before the man from Galilee and still today, were God of earth—both "over" (like Elizabeth is Queen *of* England) and "constituted by," (like chocolate is *of* cocoa)—and all the while, at the same time, God?

That's what drives this book—a nagging question that I've chased over field and stream and, once snared in my flimsy net, subjected to an experiment of the imagination. Indeed, for all that the effort might sound at first like some complicated intellectual exercise, or academic systematics, it's not. On the contrary, it's the chronicle of a question.

I guess what I'm trying to say is, this isn't a head trip; it's a journey of the heart.

So, it's also an invitation—an invitation of imagination. The implications are both ecological and personal as they blow past petrified traditions to embrace fresh questions of what Christianity might mean and be in our time.

For what is the whole Jesus-thing if not God's being of and in the material, blood, bone, and breath of it all? What is it if not a declaration of love beyond knowing for the eternal, universal Creator to take on skin and limbs and friends and grief in order to reconcile this blue-green home of ours to heaven? And what is that reconciling if not a repair that accepts the truth of our brokenness and throws a lifeline that we may grope our way toward wholeness? It's a complicated business, with weighty responsibility and a not-altogether-certain outcome, but there it is. Comfort, inspiration, and, dare I say, the possibility of hope.

If we accept the basic tenets of Christianity, then we're talking about accepting a relationship with heaven that honors the God of earth. If that sounds like turning Christianity on its head—bringing what is divine and other-worldly smack down to earth, actually *of* earth—consider this: isn't that what Christianity already does? Doesn't it turn things upside down and propose profound paradoxes even as it trumpets truth? Well. This book is an invitation to take seriously what Christian theology preaches at its most basic level: that the one eternal Creator God chose out of love to become incarnate in order to reconcile wayward human beings to God.

Some people may find this whole enterprise to be dangerously unorthodox. Yet *God of Earth* takes the most basic premises of Christian belief as its beginning and the ground from which it reaches. It reckons with the fact that even as those premises appear to be straightforward and simple, they have layers and possibilities for meaning far beyond the singular, the time-worn, and the strictly traditional.

Besides the traditional interpretations, what does it mean to think of Jesus as God of earth with the same significance as the baby in the manger, the young man with his band of a dozen friends, the crucified Christ, and the tomb-busting savior? What does it mean to imagine the incarnation of God as ever-alive and present to us in the wildly diverse and astonishingly dynamic nonhuman natural world in which we live now?

Traditional Christianity combines the time-bound, earth-stuff God who is recognized in Jesus with the timeless, universal, creator God through its calendar year, measured not January to January but Advent to Advent. As the year tracks Jesus's life, it also pushes that life back before Jesus was born and forward into the ever after. What's more, in its cyclical nature, it catapults that life beyond simply the historical event of one man to recognize a Jesus who was before, is now, and will always be. The whole point of it, according to Christianity, is a righting of wrongs, repairing what has broken, the healing of dis-ease.

There is something in the Jesus-story that issues an urgent challenge even as it gives hope. God made herself of earth to draw us into being and making right. Creator of all, God inhabited the earth within time and in a particular place in order to call to us. And God, being God to the people who follow him throughout the ever-renewing cycle of a church year, still does inhabit and call. That's the wonder of it, the terror of it, the promise of it.

If you are hurting and sad and desperately lonely in your empathy for an ailing world, I hope for you comfort. For there's something buried in the notions and humming in the interstices of the traditional metaphors that endures with renewing novelty. There is a hint of something in it that busts through despair. And I confess, sometimes I despair. I look at the rising seas and crescendoing "weather"—hurricanes, droughts, floods, and wildfires—at the hunger and extinctions and fracking and waste and pollution; I know that I participate in it, I contribute to it, and I despair.

But then there's this: God for and in . . . *of* earth.

Welcome to the journey.

PART I

Our Re-Turning Earth

"Not like my taking the veil—no solemn abjuration of the world. I only went out for a walk, and finally concluded to stay out till sundown, for going out, I found, was really going in."
—John Muir

At the tail end of November, the sidewalk is cluttered with leaves. The trees stand above it all, sober and stern, unadorned Puritans preaching the purpose of quiet rest. There's a languorous quality to the air as if it's reluctant but consigned to turn its back on summer and march dutifully into the stillness of winter. The garden's echinacea is nothing more than prickly balls atop stiff stalks that angle in complaint with each vagabond goldfinch snatching a snack as the bird passes through. The basil has shriveled to black as if cursed by the finger of the first frost, and tomato vines drape exhausted over the arms of their wire cages.

Hardly the time for beginnings, methinks. Far more sensible to start things off in spring, when life is an SPCA hound sprung from her kennel, a one-year-old pup straining at the leash to bust out in joy and utter abandon. Surely spring is the time for cosmic novelty, the time to issue an invitation of relationship irresistible to the peoples of the world—spring, with its sex and eggs and blossoms and all that.

But, no. It is late fall, a liminal moment between the memories of green summer and the knowledge that—like it or

1

not—winter's up next. It's the odd time, fall's final act, when hints and rumors of a coming God of earth whisper to attention those who might listen. Advent. It all begins with waiting, preparation . . . and more waiting.

It's a good time for a walk.

The season begins quietly, not with a sound and light show, not even with birth. In truth, given what's to come, that's a relief. After all, this is the moment when a couple of different things could happen.

Advent recognizes the coming of Jesus. But *which* Jesus— the manger baby, or the "second coming," terrifying judge of all the earth—no one yet knows. That's how tradition would have it.

We begin the season in expectation. God's incarnation, in and of earth, is coming.[1] In the spirit of this experiment, we embark on preparation, getting ready to meet either of two possible God-of-earths: earth newborn or earth in a furious reckoning. Thank goodness we've got time, weeks, to swab the decks, batten the hatches, and pray for a kindly wind.

1

Heaven, All Bound Up with Earth

"I danced in the morning when the world was begun,
and I danced in the moon and the stars and the sun."
—Sydney Carter

There is a condition, much prized in Eastern philosophy, called "beginner's mind." Despite its moniker, to attain beginner's mind and to maintain it once there takes staying power. Beginner's mind is an expert's business. It is to sustain, in the face of the accretions of experience, an openness to all possibility, a posture of cheerful wonder, the suppleness of mind to adopt and adapt to what one may never have even imagined before.

Funny the things we notice when we actually look. In the beginning, the Bible tells us, God created the heavens and the earth. Whether or not you have any experience with the Bible, that refrain echoes with a familiar ring. But listen again. Look. The story that launches the whole Bible, in which a disembodied God speaks the world into being, announces unapologetically and without explanation that what we know of heaven we know from earth.

It took me decades—until just now, truth be told—to notice this. There is no mention of heaven in Genesis 1, aside from the story's opening and conclusion. ("Sky" and "heavens" are not the same.) Rather, the heavens are all wrapped up in earth.

"God created the heavens and the earth," Genesis declares in its opening sentence. And at the end of the story, when God is done: "Thus the heavens and the earth were finished," and, "These are the generations of the heavens and the earth when they were created."[1]

Those framing statements tell as clearly as can be that Genesis 1 (and into a few verses of chap. 2) is a story of the heavens' creation just as much as it is of the earth's. Yet look. Everything in between those introductory and concluding verses is of and about the earth. Apparently, all of the ordering and establishing of earthy things—light and darkness; day and night; water here, land there; sun, moon, and stars; every being green and golden, flitting, slithering, swimming, leaping, each according to dizzyingly diverse and dynamic kinds; and wonder of wonder, the human being in its both-and-ness, male and female, the image of a creating God; and all so good, so very good—is somehow at the same time the creation of heaven, too.

The Bible is disarmingly matter-of-fact about this, declaring the creation of the heavens to be somehow what transpired in creating the stuff of earth. What we know of heaven we know from earth, the Bible suggests from its very beginning. The kingdom of heaven is indeed at hand, around us and among us. So it was created by God to be, this and other texts suggest.

This moment in the God-of-earth year is a beginning time. But to find the start, we have to go back. Look forward, and then count in reverse—December 25; then one, two, three, four Sundays back. And there it is. Here we are. The beginning of Jesus-time, the launching moment for everything that is yet to come. We stand there on the cusp of a new Spirit-soaked year, ready or not, to begin again.

I started this project with a simple question: What if the Jesus of Christian tradition were not limited to tradition but actually included earth itself? I braced myself for immediate disappointment, that such a preposterous journey would end before it even began. Yet right here, in this moment of beginnings, the tradition itself opens the door to just such an exploration.

After all, the beginning of the church year is a moment of cosmic novelty. It reminds us with each turn of the earth and each circle around the sun that the universal and eternal God, the *I AM* of all being and doing and rest, chose to become an earth-creature of blood and bone. It declares that Jesus as the incarnation of God, as God's experience of a world-bound life, inhabits time with us and like us, knows the temporality of our world—the day and night; the seasons in riotous splendor, in bounty, and in pensive containment. Jesus of the wildly free, God of all and ever, chose to be of earth in time. God of earth, year after year.

That God is in, through, and of earth, and that one cannot know God without knowing earth is a profoundly biblical notion. The earth, according to the Bible, is threaded through with thoughts of God, with the intentions of God not simply in terms of its nuts and bolts but with an inclination toward wholeness, beauty, and joy. And we human beings, created in the image of God, share in the constant responsibility and delight of realizing such goodness.

But it's a complicated business that requires great learning, attention, and care. For God and the wisdoms of the earth are connected, again according to the Bible, anyway (in both the Old Testament and the New). Wisdom was party to the origins of the world, the first of God's creative acts—present when God established the mountains and hills, the fields and the land itself—the book of Proverbs tells. And it is by wisdom that God founded the earth. What's more, Proverbs declares, wisdom is life itself; to ignore it is suicide.[2]

Wisdom, of course, is not simply an intellectual exercise but what I like to think of as knowledge with heart. Wisdom depends on information, on learning all sorts of things and in all sorts of ways; but it doesn't end there. It appreciates interconnections and dependencies in ways that naturally include both compassion and the humility of wonder.

Present at creation, *Jesus* is wisdom, is life, Christianity claims. "In the beginning, was *logos*." John's gospel opens in clear echo of Genesis 1, *logos*, the Word, as it's frequently translated.[3] But that can be misleading, because this is no ordinary word—spoken, written—as in pleasantries or on the page. It is an expression infused with the very stuff of God. In a way, it *is* God. Using such Greek, John declares that from the start of everything, *logos*, the ordering principle that charges a coming into being and infuses the creation with a wisdom of its own, was there. This Word, this *logos*, John says, was with God, *was* God. *Logos* is Jesus, "the Word made flesh."

In the beginning, when God first brought the stuff of earth into being in rightness and order, wisdom was there. Just as God spoke the world into being and it was good, so all that being is infused with the wisdom of divine articulation—the *logos*, the Word, the God-of-Earth Christ. So it was in the beginning. Such was the condition into which everything came to be. In and through, by and by the Word was each and every thing.

Such is the quality of beginning, the Bible tells—Emmanuel, God with us, divine wisdom and order, here on and in earth. In the beginning, the Bible tells, was God. And from the beginning God was interested in earth, invested in earth. God was of earth.

So it begins. Again. The year has chased itself round to start again. For those who've been riding the wheel of traditional Jesus-time, who observe the Christian liturgical calendar, it is time to slough off the old—failures to follow the risen Christ, wrestling to locate the Jesus of the previous season beyond gender and age, in the mundane and sublime—and to leave it behind. Here on the first day of the new, the mature Jesus of our days in work and rest, politics and entertainment, family and foreigner gives way to the Jesus not-yet, to possibilities radicalized in the Word made flesh.

For the rest of us who haven't paid much attention to the church season or contemplated time in the context of Jesus, it's a beginning at least as profound. The beginning of this Jesus-beyond-Jesus-time is an invitation to make room for the wonder of God in earth and to celebrate its implications for justice, for beauty, for peace, for ecological sustainability, for correction, direction, and joy.

The candle for the beginning of Advent, the beginning of the liturgical year, is associated with hope. And why not? What is more definitive of beginnings than possibility, and with possibility—the as yet unmade business of the future—hope. Maybe that's why we keep beginning, to keep alive the hope for what's to come—that we may be better, that it may be good.

So it is, some weeks before the God of earth even arrives, that we begin. Creation and novelty. A new heaven and a new earth *adventus*, is "coming."

2

Preparing, and the Terror of Uncertainty

"If you want to attract lightning bugs, the best thing to plant is nothing."

—James Lloyd

Scientists tell us to expect a flood of refugees commensurate with literal floods to come. A recent report from the World Bank based on a collection of scientific studies warns of famine in sub-Saharan Africa, where an increase of only 1.5 to 2 degrees Celsius could lead in the next decade or two to a loss of 40 to 80 percent of cropland. In Southeast Asia, rising salt water "of 30 cm, possible by 2040 if business as usual continues," will ruin crops in Vietnam's Mekong Delta, which provides rice around the world; Bangladesh, Kolkata, and Mumbai will see massive cyclones and disruptions in the monsoon season with enormous population-displacing floods.[1] Never mind that Venice may be lost, expensive American beachfront under water, and Manhattan an ever smaller island as stoic glaciers finally succumb, and the ocean swirls their molecules away. Increasingly devastating droughts will pummel dry land, while a terrible sky elsewhere will pour torrents unrelenting. Will this be the year?

We are right to be afraid. And yet, not yet.

People are also wising up, taking responsible action. Insulation in cold climes has become de rigueur, many Millennials opt for smaller houses nearer their work, and I keep getting requests to buy the old Prius that my dad passed along to me years ago. Trees continue growing, inhaling carbon dioxide; buffalo with their good stewardship of streams and prairies are ambling back in the West; and some of our native birds and spiders have finally decided to eat the Asian stinkbugs that over the past several years had blanketed windows, crept into book bindings, and fallen helplessly, impossibly onto the pastry cream of my husband's birthday tart.

Uncertainty is unsettling, and downright terrifying at times. Preparation can be an antidote. In the case of Advent, it isn't so much a readiness to deal with particulars as a readying of one's self, one's manner, one's heart for whatever's to come. That, I submit, is also the active recalibration of our habits and assumptions in order to slow, if not arrest, our devastating effects on the planet.

As Christians await the coming of Jesus, they cannot know in this moment if he will be the take-no-prisoners judge of Revelation or the sweet baby of Luke's crude manger. Christian tradition dictates that at this point in the season, one's preparation be for a coming of two kinds—for Jesus's second coming as well as his first. It is not only to prepare for the sweet child in the manger, cooing and oohing among the animals, chubby hands held out in blessing from his mother's arms. Preparation is also for the awe-ful Jesus, risen and come to judge the living and dead. Hence the liturgy's biblical readings from texts such as Matthew 24 of Jesus coming "like a thief in the night," of trimming one's lamp, and of Noah's flood. For the not-yet Jesus of Advent is both the newborn God and the risen-now-returning Christ.

By analogy with the God of earth, we can hope in this time for a healing earth. But we face also the terms and limits of a mature earth fed up with our folly and demanding a reckoning. Even as we have committed acts for which the earth calls us to account (via climate change, for example), we can hope that with new hearts and minds we may get another chance to do better (with positive ecological effects). It's right, appropriate, for us to experience anxiety in the uncertainty about which

God of earth (like which Jesus—a baby, or a judge) is coming. We must get ready for either.

So, preparation at this point for the God of earth is undertaken with both eagerness and terror, anticipation of judgment and anticipation of joy. It involves renewed attendance to the delight of what is sweet, generous, and fresh, to the possibility that we may yet get it right; and at the same time, respect for natural power beyond our control, recognizing the effects and corrections of the earth in the face of unsustainable endeavors, and allowing that we may be in for a devastating punishment.

How do we prepare? There is the meditative, contemplative preparation of heart and soul as prescribed by tradition. And it has a counterpoint in the context of the God of earth—taking time to reflect how we are in relation to the world around us, the ways that we want to be and feel that we should be vis-à-vis the nonhuman natural world. But preparation doesn't end there. Research and musing lead to correction, an effort to get our proverbial house in order before the God of earth arrives. To make less fossil-fuel dependent choices in daily life; to make space for what is wild; and to take delight in the nonmaterial goods of friendship, art, and family—these also are concrete acts of preparation for the coming God of earth, whichever one arrives.

Around this time of year, we hear much lamenting within Christian communities about how we've lost the spiritual richness of the season with its demands and pleasures, that we've rejected the religious heart of it. "Put Christ back into Christmas" is a common refrain. But within the annual Christmas rounds of cookies and booze, in the face of the angst—what to get for the in-laws, where to place the ornament from an ex, how to keep the turkey when the fridge is already stuffed—in the context of securing the tree, stringing the lights, baking, cleaning, and dusting off the Christmas CDs, how does one prepare for the coming of God?

It's easy to chide ourselves for superficiality, a loss of focus on the heart of the season. And there's some justification for that, of course. But I don't think it's a given that all these aspects of the season are necessarily without spiritual merit. All this preparation and celebration, so easy to dismiss as secularizing and flattening the true meaning of Christmas, just may hold rich goodness themselves. They can be proper preparation for the coming God of earth.

Ironically, what passes for preparation in this secular form can be the meeting place for the traditional religious Advent and for the coming God of earth. In the so-called secular stuff, preparing for a traditional Jesus and preparing for a God of earth can come together to redefine the whole enterprise. But it requires intention.

Take gift-giving. To get out of one's own head, one's own wanting and wishing, and attend rather to the needs and desires of others is a good and right reorientation of the sort that prepares us for the coming of the God of earth. Part of our preparation for the not-yet-Jesus, not-yet-God-of-earth is this expectation that we would think of others.

What's more, we can select gifts that themselves give—in support of a local craftsperson, to promote sustainable agriculture, provide fun ways for a child to learn math, simply to stretch the imagination, or in celebration of beauty. Isn't this also to prepare the way for God? The God of the beginning, who invested the earth with order and wisdom, charged us in our male-female humanness to have dominion over a good creation. Surely making or selecting for others something special that does no harm to the world and may even be good qualifies as preparation for the coming Christ, the God of earth.

As for the other—the decoration, the cards, the rounds of food and drink—why can't they also be in preparation for the coming of God herself? Delight and pleasure, all in "good spirit," for goodness sakes, reconnecting friends distanced by jobs and family and the daily grind, reintroducing people estranged through miles and mistakes and grudges long held— surely these also raise the valleys, straighten the roads, and level out the rutted and ridged to make a way for the coming of God, as John the Baptist put it (echoing the prophet Isaiah).[2] And in the process, when undertaken with an intention to do least harm, we prepare for the God of earth.

We've been accustomed to thinking of ecological issues as isolated from or even competing with other issues of concern—social, economic, international—but they're not. We're finally waking up to the fact that what harms the environment inevitably undermines human health and welfare, has costly ramifications, and is never site-specific but global in reach. In preparing for the coming God of earth, the exercise of delight in the company of others, in the aesthetic of our space, and in good food and drink, can all be just as relevant as traditional, "religious" Christmas preparations.

And what if we expand the notion of company to include the presence of nonhuman beings in our lives? That includes pets, of course, but also the birds that come to the feeder, the row of sycamore along the drive, the overwintering rosemary, the turtles hibernating deep in the silt under the frozen pond, and the centuries old oak near the airport up the road, not to mention beings far, far away who are nevertheless affected by our choices. And why can't the delight of decorations include the way a shrub looks under snow, a bright cardinal in the branches, the stark beauty of bare limbs against a winter sky? We prepare for the coming God of earth also by taking such joy. To plan, to prepare, and to enjoy the food and drink of our place, recognizing and selecting what promotes the livelihood of others with as little a carbon footprint as possible, this too prepares for the coming God of earth.

Finally, preparation may also mean being intentional about hope. This is especially challenging for me. It seems we are a world of foolish virgins, squandering the earth without a thought for tomorrow, without a thought for dire consequences that if not we, then the most vulnerable of society and our children and grandchildren will have to bear (not to mention all those individuals of all those species other than human). Yet we are called in these weeks of preparation also to hope, called to confidence that the newborn God of earth will usher in green life, the peace of balance, and joy. Perhaps we trim our lamps and prepare for the coming God as much by keeping the faith that something may actually tilt the change for good or by being intentional about joy, about beauty and truth, about delight, as by living with as little destruction to the earth as possible. Perhaps.

3

Waiting, On Becoming Expert in Humility

"Nature does not hurry, yet everything is accomplished."
—Lao Tzu

The box cover was glossy. Darling pink creatures with tiny hands and feet, cavorting in their aqua blue home, suspended in a weightless world, happy grins on sweet faces. Some wore tiny crowns—princes and princesses. Others swam around the castle attending to whatever was required in this wonderful sea monkey kingdom. They were fantastic. And they were mine.

I had begged my parents to buy the kit. There it was, in the local pet store, where we bought guppies and goldfish food. They had no fur, I cajoled, nothing to send my allergy-afflicted sisters to the hospital (though I was perfectly ready to trade those sisters for a dog). The brochure touted how the sea monkeys responded to you. They could be trained. They even liked to follow you around. I was ecstatic when my parents shelled out the cost. Back home, my dad helped me to set things up. It was all so easy. The final step was to pour, ever so gently, the packet of actual creatures into the water. "Then," my dad said, "we wait."

This was not something I'd counted on. The "creatures" floated, dried and lifeless as winter leaves on the surface of the water. My dad assured me that this was simply part of the process. After the allotted time, in our carefully prepared "sea," they would come to life. But I'd been so excited. How could I possibly wait? Understand, of my failings (and there are many), I was not a tantrum-throwing kind of kid. But there, in the living room of our old ranch rambler, I lost it. I gave in to a full-blown tantrum of epic proportions. What do you mean, wait? I could not possibly wait.

Halfway into this first season is a nadir of sorts. We launched the new year with all the freshness of beginning, engaged in the hard and happy work of preparing; but the big moment still has not arrived. It's not even particularly close. This is the dull point, the hard time, the neither beginning nor there-yet time. The God of earth is coming, sure, but isn't yet even just around the bend. There is nothing a soul can do at this point but wait.

But what could be less interesting, less inspiring than waiting? It's a silly, old-fashioned notion, anyway. Who waits for anything these days? Netflix and movies on demand, the microwave, cell phones, airplanes, and Instagram. Waiting is for luddites and nostalgia junkies. The rest of us just get on with it. Or not. Hang on.

Even in the face of all the insta-everything, there are some things for which we still and nevertheless must wait. The most profound, irrefutable, and basic of these have to do with life. The best bread cannot be rushed. The little life bugs of microscopic yeast cells must have time to do their work. Same goes for wine, tomatoes, and a tree. As for a baby, it cannot even *be* without time, and in that time, the blood and breath and food and bones that its mother's body, without argument or question or negotiation, provides. For a baby, one must wait. Mother Mary, full of grace.

This first season dictates that we wait. But most of us are no good at waiting anymore. The experts tend to be inferiors, humble, and in some way poor. The ones who wait are children for attention, patients for doctors, wild things for prey or peace. The ones who wait are parents for a car-driving teen out at night, dogs chained in the rain, fishermen for fish. No one wants to be experienced in waiting. Waiting is thrust upon us.

Waiting is at its core a humbling thing. It presumes another to whom or on which one is obliged or even dependent. Those who are in charge don't wait. They call the shots, determine the action, make the choices. To wait is to be subservient. Oh, we can find things to do in the meantime—read a book while waiting for a friend, take a walk while waiting for a call on the totable cell, peruse magazines in the grocery line while waiting for the coupon-clipper ahead of us, weed the garden while waiting for the cucumbers to plump. But still, when waiting, a part of us is not our own.

The *adventus* of the God of earth in this hang-on, not-yet time coaches us in the rigorous work that is waiting, work that readies us for the arrival of God. To wait is its own form of preparation, a preparation of the soul for the coming of God.

For all of the many differences between religious traditions and beliefs, one thing they share in common is a requirement to get outside of oneself, to put something or someone ahead of the *self*, to focus elsewhere than on the *me*—if no more than simply to recognize that I am part of a much greater whole. The act of waiting puts us into just such a position, whether we like it or not. It reminds us, often uncomfortably, that some things are outside of our control. Things or beings that we cannot dictate, completely determine, or manage affect us. God, for instance. Sometimes, all we can do in the face of that fact is wait.

Waiting is different from resting. Waiting has an energy of its own. It presumes attendance and attention. It's a kind of action, even as it is a forced inaction. Before John Milton wrote *Paradise Lost*, he went blind. The sonnet "On His Blindness," a poem that Milton composed before he would write that great epic, is a poignant question about self-worth and expectation in the face of such disability. "Doth God exact day-labour light denied?" Milton asks. He reflects on Jesus's parable of the talents—how each of three employees managed the sum of money that his absenting employer left in his care. The story tells of using, not keeping, of spending, not hiding, the resources. But how to do that, Milton asks, when a writer is blind, when "that one talent . . . is lodged within me useless?" It is Patience who answers him. Simply to "bear his mild yoke" is not only service enough; it is to serve God best of all. Finally, Milton concludes, "They also serve who only stand and wait."

To wait is to refrain, to restrain oneself. Ours is a society that praises action and abundance. We call the explosion of industry "progress" and the proliferation of suburbs with strip malls and highways and streetlights and filling stations "development." Yet our hope for a future closer to the care and keeping that Yahweh-God assigned to the first human being lies more in restraint. We do well to practice waiting, then— waiting for, waiting on.

And waiting is relational. On the surface, we might seem to be doing nothing; but inside, we are preoccupied with the reason for our waiting, with the one on whom we wait. We think about the object of our waiting—the daughter, the husband, the friend, the plums to ripen, the rare bird to come into view, the baby to come. "Those who wait on the LORD shall renew their strength, they shall mount up with wings like eagles," Isaiah says.[1] When it comes to God, waiting on/for her is itself sustaining and empowering, the biblical text promises.

Waiting on and for the God of earth brings all these qualities to bear—the humble recognition that God can be in and through the world around us in ways that we do not control but that affect us deeply; the exercise of paying attention to the earth, noticing its ways and respecting its value independent of our selves; and simply being still in the face of it all, holding back from imposing ourselves in busy-ness and change to wait, instead, with keen attendance for the wonder that Jesus as the God of earth might bring.

The sea monkeys were a disappointment. They were simply brine shrimp, after all. Sure, they went where I directed—with a flashlight—but most of them didn't survive to do even that. Yet by the time it mattered, I was on to something else. I'd lost interest altogether. But I've never forgotten the trauma of waiting, my fury in the face of expectations denied.

The God of earth is uncompromising about the terms and conditions of natural processes. We can stamp our feet and wail in protest, but a five-hundred-year-old redwood cannot be cut down one afternoon and grow to the same grandeur in the next. The rich soil of America's heartland, the product of millennia of wildly diverse prairies, cannot be refashioned in industrial factories, masterminded by suits in skyscrapers, no matter how many tech wizards toil in basement labs. And mountain gorillas cannot persist in their magnificent selves without time and the proper space to form healthy communities unassaulted by human beings. Meanwhile, the lichen on a Canadian island, lichen as persistent as it is silent, masticates the granite on which it lives, eventually and ever so slowly producing the tablespoon of soil out of which who-knows-what will grow—lacy columbine, a curmudgeonly jack pine, blueberries? And so we wait.

4

Anticipation

"Here . . . there is always reserve and mystery, always something beyond, on earth and sea something which nature, honouring, conceals."

—Henry Beston

It was a big night for us—dinner *and* a show. One of our favorite stand-up comedians, Lewis Black, had come to town. We made reservations for a lovely little restaurant downtown, took some time to gussy up. The opener wrapped up his act, and finally Black walked on stage. When the applause died down, Black took the microphone and advised that everyone should now just go home. Black draws gigantic laughs for observing and articulating the universal experience of anticipation.

After the beginning and the preparation, the hard strain of waiting finally gives way to anticipation. Anticipation is waiting infused with confidence. Energized, it's waiting jazzed on a triple shot of espresso. Anticipation is the surety that whatever one has looked forward to, whether with trepidation or eagerness, is just around the corner. It is coming soon. "There's no better moment," Black said, "than the moment when you're anticipating what the f-ing moment's going to be." Anticipation.

Most of the time, Black may be right. But in the case of the mystical, spiritual, supernatural, I disagree. There's a categorically different quality, determined by what we bring to the moment—by belief and our willingness to accept the invitation extended. It's an attitude thing. In the case of the God of earth, this final period of waiting is when hope becomes concrete, when waiting is colored with the confidence of expectation. God has chosen, again, to be with us and for us through all the wonder of earth itself.

In the traditional Christian story, finally the uncertainty is gone. Now we know that the days of waiting will lead to the manger, not the super-cosmic Jerusalem of John's apocalypse. In terms of the God of earth, it's when we know that the incarnation of God will be of a kind inviting and full of promise, rather than the exacting terror of a reckoning earth.

Because finally, Mary conceives. Sure, the church marks an annunciation back in March; but within the traditional calendar of biblical readings for Advent, Mary's conception is recalled only days before Christmas. (Alternatively, either the story of Joseph's learning of Mary's pregnancy or the story of the pregnant Elizabeth meeting the pregnant Mary is read.)

At first blush, it seems odd that this should happen on the final Sunday in Advent, not on the first. And yet. The biblical texts tell and the traditional Christian calendar maintains that the living God for whom we have been waiting all these long weeks was in and of the world before Mary ever was. The Jesus of Christian tradition and faith is God incarnate—the *logos* who was in the beginning, is now and ever shall be. Jesus existed before Mary's pregnancy, and that living God endures still after Mary's son had been executed. God's engagement with earth predated the historical Jesus-event and endures, believers claim, still today. That there are weeks of Advent before Mary even conceived makes perfect sense, then, or at least makes its own kind of sense.

But what of earth itself? How does that work in thinking about God's becoming not only human but somehow mysteriously and miraculously taking on the flesh of earth itself, born of and into this entire, great, blue-green planet home of ours? It would mean that the material machinations of the nonhuman natural world around us, with its own birthing, living, and dying, its structures, laws, and evolution become infused anew by nothing less than God, who in becoming of earth subjects God's self to all of what we associate traditionally with Jesus.

It is to imagine that the divine Creator's intention is to become realized in the stuff and doing of the soil and the rain and the trees and the fishes and the birds as they are all connected in a vast web of life, *in order that we may become right with God.*

So now we know for sure: the one coming is Jesus meek and mild, a baby without teeth or speech, continence or reason; not the terrible Jesus of Revelation with eyes like flames of fire and feet of burnished bronze, in whose mouth is a sword, and whose head and hair are white as wool.[1]

In this final period of waiting for the coming God of earth, we anticipate that moment of the infusion into earth of a loving God intent on redemption. We lean in to the hope of earth transformed—from a material mass of the profane to a sacred vitality yearning to heal every rift, within and without, in holy wholeness . . . to give life abundant.

Advent comes at the time of year when we most crave light, when for us in the Northern Hemisphere (where traditional Christianity took shape), the days are short and the nights last ever so long. So too Jesus, as the God of earth, whose coming is oh-joy-soon inhabits in these days the darkness of a womb, subterranean darkness, the darkness of ocean depths, the darkness of night.

I grew up in northern Minnesota the child of Swedish Americans, whose very bones remember the darkness of winter. Depression runs deep and wide in my family. For all that, it's a state of being that doesn't preclude joy or laughter or hope. We seize levity and delight with fierce energy. Darkness bears like an ache, inside and out, which makes light in winter dear indeed.

It was dark in the morning when I set out with my friend Naira, our books on our backs, for the trek to school. And it was already dusk after school when I skied cross-country in the long twilight, its rosy violet a heartbreaking tenderness. The darkness seemed to last forever. Then one morning in December, my mother would grin at me in the kitchen of her childhood, too. "Guess what?" she would ask. Then, too excited to wait, "The days are getting longer!" she'd say. Born and raised in that town on the tip of Lake Superior, my mother had internalized its seasons. She marked the solstice, kept track of the darkness, and celebrated an imperceptible turn to the light.

Is it any wonder that the role of light should be so great in this Jesus-time moment? Jesus, bringer of light and life. Jesus's life, the Gospel of John tells, was light itself, the true light and the light of all people. "The light shines in the darkness, and the darkness did not overcome it."[2]

But what does it mean to bring light if there isn't any darkness? Can we even know light without darkness? "Our civilization has fallen out of touch with night," Henry Beston writes, "With lights, we drive the holiness and beauty of night back."[3]

We have confused a metaphorical darkness with the literal.

It is right to celebrate the light, good to mark its many benefits. But in our world, in our present historical and geographical context, where we control our environment without giving that power a second thought, we forget the value of darkness. The biblical texts, even the Christmas carols that we sing, come from times and places very different from our own. Back then—decades, centuries, and millennia past—exercising as much control over one's environment as possible was crucial to survival and didn't ensure it even then, so minimally could people affect the greater nonhuman natural world.

Today, we hardly even know what darkness is. We light up everything, all the time. The ambient light from gas stations, shopping malls, neighborhoods, billboards, and buildings of all kinds has created a round-the-clock twilight nearly everywhere on earth. Few of us know anymore what it's like to step out at night unable to see the ground, the trees, our houses. We have forgotten how to let our eyes adjust, to follow sound, to walk slowly and lightly, to look up at the stars. We sleep with the glow of electronics by the bedside, walk beneath streetlights, flip a switch in the bathroom, and find a midnight snack by the refrigerator's auto glow.

And it all comes with a cost. Besides the expense to the environment of generating that electricity, all this light, this light all the time just isn't good—not for the animals, insects, fish and birds, and not for us. Darkness affords the liberty of hiddenness, hence its association with crime. But hiddenness is also the condition out of which new things begin—the darkness of the womb, of the mud, the cocoon, the cave, of ocean depths below. Darkness is a primal necessity.

We need it to achieve the most restorative stages of sleep, of course. But darkness also heightens our creaturely senses. It requires that we pay a different kind of attention. Sound and smell, touch and even taste amplify without the distraction of looking and seeing. In darkness is quiet and humility, too. To keep from stepping on the dog or tripping on the rug, running into a tree, or stepping into a hole, one must move slowly. To hear in the dark, one must be quiet, one must be still.

Darkness unsettles us, and it puts us back together again. Even apart from the fear of a real danger in the dark—the rapist, the thief—when I find myself in utter darkness, my heart pounds more quickly, my breath is shallow. Until I can settle down, I am afraid. But is this so bad? To let go into the darkness, slow one's breath, and allow the space around to have no definition, no shape or sense, can be finally centering. And is it so bad to be afraid? Yes, if it's in the face of a bullying brutality. But is it so bad to experience the fear that recalls to us our insufficiencies, shows up our vulnerability, makes us reckon with something greater than ourselves? Can we appreciate the moment of God's inhabiting the world if we do not know how desperately the world needs what is sacred, beautiful, and true?

"The fear of Yahweh-God is the beginning of understanding" lies at the heart of biblical wisdom literature. The Hebrew word translated "fear" in this context means awe. If we steep ourselves in the darkness of the days before Christmas, before God becomes of earth, before Jesus is born, we can open ourselves to the awesome wonder of a God who intends to be with us, among us, of us. Then, we put our hands to our mouths and squinch our eyes shut in anticipation. For the one of old, from ancient times, through whom all was made, in whom is darkness as well as life and light, who bound holiness to our humanity, and who requires everything, is on the way. In such darkness, fear strikes the match of understanding.

The God of earth, the incarnation of what is true and right and good inhabits the darkness as well as the light. What if the God for whom we wait in this winter of the year brings to us true darkness along with or even rather than light? Out of darkness, the God of earth comes.

PART II

God, New-Born

"Nature is too thin a screen; the glory of the omnipresent God bursts through everywhere."

—Ralph Waldo Emerson

Hiking through the High Sierras with a flock of marauding sheep, John Muir happened upon a field of magnificent lilies, some up to eight feet tall. Nothing surrounded them in protection or warning. There was no natural barrier to their exquisite flowers. They grew simply, available for any and all. "So extravagant is Nature with her choicest treasures," Muir exclaimed, "spending plant beauty as she spends sunshine . . . the beauty of lilies falls on angels and men, bears and squirrels, wolves and sheep, birds and bees."[1]

What an outrageous act of God choosing to be born into the world, choosing to be of the world. In the spirit of this experiment, hear in Muir's "Nature" God, the God of earth, a Jesus beyond Jesus. What an audacious thing, irresponsible even, to cast something of such inestimable value, and vulnerable, too, out into the world for any and all.

For our part, we have a choice: to live and move about within the nonhuman natural world in respectful relationship, or to reject the invitation and treat the earth as nothing more than a resource for our use and disposal. Muir marvels that "awkward lumbering bears . . . and deer with their sharp feet" lounge and traipse without spoiling a single lily. And he laments the propensity that human beings and our domesticated animals have to damage and destroy.

To greet the world with new eyes, eyes that see it not as a mere mass of inert material—sometimes interesting, occasionally lovely, but ultimately of value only as it conforms to our commerce—and rather instead as the newborn incarnation of an extravagantly generous God bent on redemption is a complicating proposition. For even as we celebrate Jesus's birth with deck-the-halls joy, we accept a certain responsibility to care for the tender newborn, to sacrifice in honor of its holiness, and to protect against the despoiling Herods of our time. It isn't easy, and as the year later recalls, we will fail. But for now, there is joy, and to the manger of this new earth we bring adoration and love.

The church traditionally calls this time Christmas and Epiphany. (Yes, they're yoked as one.) It's the dawning of God's incarnation in the world—a recognition that spreads from a tiny circle of beings, human and nonhuman alike, to the political power of the day and internationally.

Nights of a jagged cold but clear, as clear often follows heavy snow where I come from. The temperatures drop and the stars hang like shards of water frozen, suspended in a velvet sky. This is the time to go out. A big moon, extravagant if full, illuminates the earth and makes of snowy branches a sterling calligraphy inviting those with wool to wear and a will to see to come and wander, hush in the stillness. A fresh start, a chance to do better, a reason to hope.

5

Our Awesome, Fragile World, Instructions Not Included

"God made everything out of nothing. But the nothingness shows through."

—Paul Valéry

Forget everything you've ever heard about Christmas, forget everything you've heard about Christianity for that matter, and consider this: The cellular wisdom of dynamic nature (what makes a rose smell like a rose and guides giraffes to evolve long necks), the energy of weather both relieving and terrifying, the urge to love and be loved, the source of all stories and art and surprise, the architect of death and keeper of mystery—that which both contains and transcends everything, the only One worthy of all worship through all time—became of earth-stuff one day, undeniably small, and absolutely vulnerable.

Why? To reconcile the heavens with earth. And what of the before-time? There was no before-time. It's always been like this—always the rending and always the repair—the heavens created in the stuff of earth, and the humans (created in God's image to rule and care and tend) always messing up. But what of that day? Sure, it's a moment in time. But it's an eternal and ever-renewing moment. We acknowledge its happening each year again and again. This is the season of the birth of the God of earth.

The word "nature" comes from the Latin *nasci*, "to be born." If there's something all newborns share, it is their sheer dependence. Good thing, then, that babies elicit delight, joy, tenderness, and adoration simply by being. A baby brings out in us the qualities necessary for care. Those qualities are the same for the earth as for an infant. We are responsible for a baby's well-being. To that end, we pay close attention, let our own wants and needs take second place, and enjoy the beauty and surprise that the newborn brings. In the case of God, why should the nature of being newborn be any different?

Some years ago, I attended the lecture of a colleague who gave Christmas a different slant than I'd ever considered before.[1] A father again late in life, he reflected on the business of babies—their inherent helplessness and the lengths that we go to in order to provide for their welfare, safety, and happiness. Of course. We do everything for children, and for babies, even more. After all, infants cannot articulate even their most basic needs. We adults have to listen and guess, to pay attention often fiercely, sometimes frustratingly, to determine what they want, what they need. We delight in their pleasure and sometimes simply gaze at them, adoring. Babies demand full attention and all of our energy. We fetch them things, smile when they do, and weep with exhaustion at their impossible demands. We kiss their feet.

Well played, God. To come to earth and be of earth, not as a gigantic dictator, not as a volcano, a great white whale, celebrity princess, or hurricane—but as a baby. Stroke of genius.

But I fear that we've missed the truth of it, preoccupied as we are with a literal Bethlehem (in Palestine, six miles south of Jerusalem), a manger (or was it a cave?), Mother Mary (and about that virgin thing . . .). Obsessed with historical details, we miss the cosmic and timeless nature of it. I'm not against the celebration of a Middle-Eastern boy born two thousand years ago; but if that's a moment of God's incarnation, as Christianity would have it—divinity becoming of earth—then it is universal and ahistorical in its implications. In terms of this book, the attention, love, and care that the baby Jesus draws forth from us by his very nature as a poor infant is the same as earth's—to attend, to care, to take delight, and to worry over the earth is to worship the newborn God.

So it is that this season is for the ones who serve. It is for those who contain their strength, tame their fury, mummy wrap a primal power in order to be for quietness and care. Christmas is for mothers and other animals—the horse who stands unmoving over a rider thrown unconscious; the buffalo in a circle around their young; the dog who follows the wandering toddler; the mother whose body, burdened and torn, made and brought forth another.

A newborn Jesus makes us consider as at no other point in the year those whose lives are defined by others—Mary, the donkey, the sheep. O come, all ye faithful. A newborn doesn't arrive from nowhere. She doesn't hitch a Greyhound or pursue a vocation. A newborn is intimately, fundamentally dependent (for coming into being and for its life apart) on its mother. And the baby's mother is, the moment of her infant's arrival, at her most vulnerable, too. Labor and birth are the most physically traumatic experiences that a human being naturally accepts.

This is what Christmas Day elicits from us, then—the containment of our potential, the restraint of our power and abilities, the control of our furies. Not for its own sake but for the sake of God, a radically vulnerable newborn who has thrown God's self into our arms, gambling everything on our care. We rein in all those outward impulses—the getting and spending, the building and pushing and amassing and making—to focus on what is here now, to pay attention for the moments of a newborn's most vulnerable time, on ensuring the baby's survival. In the process, we are torn, rent open, and vulnerable in realizing a newborn God of earth. Yet with excruciating effort comes joy.

We return to our work and advancement only after ensuring that the baby is fine, and we do so with that effort in mind. Having paid attention, close and careful; having taken joy and delight from the soft skin, the wordless speech delivered with abandon, even the naked fear and sleeplessness; our work is different, informed by care for another practiced in looking closely for what is best. It's the earth I'm talking about here as much as anything else, as much as a boy-child born some two thousand years ago or a daughter born today. For if one considers the theology of it—God's becoming of earth to reconcile us to God's self, then that's one of the implications of this great story.

On Christmas Day, we are invited to the humble place where God is new and needing. We are invited to practice thinking and caring for what is not *me* or even *us*, to rethink how we are in the world, how our doing affects the welfare of a world inhabited by God who at this moment needs for us to pay attention, and out of that attention to create the conditions of health and security at the manger (which is everywhere, of course). There is joy in it and delight. Paying close attention, we see how a black swallowtail butterfly depends on the parsley, and bats undisturbed will clear a yard of mosquitoes, how trout spawn in fresh-flowing rivers, the sweetness of a raspberry in season, and the satisfaction of walking to where one needs to go.

We *can* do otherwise, and we will. We will make compromises and fall on our faces. We will fly in airplanes and hole up in office buildings. We will construct new homes and eat foods shipped from far away. We will train troops and give them guns, make dams, dig out and cut down what people will pay for, and we will burn things. Some of our actions will promote harmony in the world, many will come with a new set of problems, and most we won't be sure of until after we've had to decide.

The manger is a reorienting place. It isn't right to stay there forever. But it is wrong never to go, never to recognize a holiness among us, never to contemplate (really contemplate with singular attention for a real amount of time) how best to secure life and health and joy. It is wrong never to delight in wonder or to laugh simply because the God of earth smiled. It is wrong never to find a place for restraint, a time to control our ambitions, a reason to kneel and adore.

I love Christmas carols. Music allows a theology that neither the best preaching nor the most comprehensive and erudite writing can touch. Christmas carols usher us in the back door and feed us grilled cheese at the kitchen table. While fancy philosophy and sophisticated theology build multistoried columns, a fabulous front porch with elegant double doors freshly painted and bedecked with red-ribbon wreaths, songs simply prop open the ragged screen out back. Singing our lungs out (or simply attending, listening with care), we tromp in with our muddy boots and our ravenous hunger, only to find ourselves effortlessly, wonderfully, before the manger, fed.

O come, all ye faithful. Invitation and celebration. We are both host and guest. "O come." We spread out our arms in welcome. "Come," we say, from the front door in our velvet and tails. "Come," we call in apron and jeans from the back. "Come, ye faithful," you who believe that God could be of and in earth to offer hope that the world might be repaired. "Come," too, to those who *would* believe, who yearn for hope, who want to know that all is not lost, that we haven't so damaged the planet, its creatures, and each other that death is the only future. On this day, we smile wide, throw open the doors and sing, "O come."

We are hosts. But we are also guests.

We do not have to be in charge, manage and orchestrate the manner of praise, the shape of witness. "Let's go. Let's see for ourselves." For on the birth day of the God of earth, we also simply join the throng of those who wish to see the newborn redeemer, to witness the reality of holiness in earth, truth and beauty in rude country, and peace. O come ye, O come we, people of modern times with modern preoccupations, all the concerns and opportunities of our time—come. The manger is here. The morning is now, we sing.

Carols bring a past rushing forward to permeate the present with the timelessness of God. They are not merely nostalgic recollections of long ago but use the language of eternal present. "O come," we sing with others, "let's see for ourselves." "O come," we pray to God, "be born in us today." In the air all around, out of the terrifying rush of angel wings rings declaration of the eternal creator present in earth, through earth, of earth. But be not afraid. God is a baby. Come. Come and behold her, born the king of angels. A new day—hope, joy, triumph—is here.

And boy, do I need it. I confess I buckle at times to the weight of despair. I worry that the worst qualities of human nature are getting the upper hand in greed, laziness, and unchecked narcissism. Worry morphs into a bleak confidence that there is no way that we will ever right our planet's balance, that too few people even know that it's out of whack, and that the ones who can do most care least of all. With a sadness that goes deeper than words, I shrug in grief for today's children and their children, deprived of wildness, of diversity, pure water one can take for granted, and air breathed freely without concern. My eyes smart for the nonhuman critters who suffer deprivations, confusion, loss, and tremendous pain in the face of our mismanagement. I know that despair is its own kind of sin. But sometimes I'm right there, guilty as charged.

Then this moment comes with hope and joy. Whatever else the year in its cycles brings, whatever our actions in time have wrought, on Christmas, when God is new on earth and of earth, hope exists. "Joyful and triumphant." We can go to the place, behold and adore. Whatever else we may believe, think, calculate, and conclude, on Christmas, in this moment, we can simply bask in the wonder of a newborn God of earth. Nothing else is required, only recognition and praise. To adore preempts everything else. Heart-heavy grief, pessimism born of seeing some inexorable march of ignorance and greed, the trauma of animals disenfranchised and abused, all are still there but there is this: the joy of God come to earth. "Sing in exultation!" God is in and of earth.

"Yea, Lord we greet thee, born this happy morning." *This* morning is Christmas morning, the moment when God reveals God's self to us again—not in thundering judgment, not as some heavenly spirit with impossible demands but as being of earth. "Word of the Father now in flesh appearing," the carol sings. "God's Word"—the instruction, intelligence, and intention of God the Creator, parent of all—appears new on this day as earth-stuff itself. O come, let us adore him. Let us adore her. Let us adore the male-female incarnation of the God who created, sustains, and remains (wonder of wonder) deeply committed to a relationship with us of earth.

I lived in Boston for a time and walked all over the place. One of my favorite routes took me through Copley Square, past Trinity Church and the statue of Phillip Brooks, the pastor who wrote "O, Little Town of Bethlehem, / How still we see thee lie." Brooks wrote "we," where he could just as easily and some would argue more accurately write to situate the song's events two thousand years ago. After all, that's when Jesus was born, right? Yet Brooks chose "we." And he chose "the hopes and fears of all the years are met in thee tonight." Tonight. It makes my throat ache. The song makes Bethlehem Every-where and the place of Christ's birth any human heart. The "holy child of Bethlehem" is no historically preserved, nostalgic notion, but the "blessing of heaven," the God of earth.

Much has been made of the heart as manger, of making ourselves more compassionate for the sick, generous to the poor, more committed to making peace on earth. All of that is good and important. But this is not merely a God of humankind. This is the God of earth, capable of exorcising the worst from ourselves and quietly, silently, entering in to "be born in us today." This is prayer. Let our innards be the manger where the newborn God of earth rests his downy head. Let our minds, our hearts, our muscles and nerves, bones and blood be the place where she is born.

This is the God of all—not only all of humanity but of all-all. God became material earth stuff dependent on the ecosystems of earth for nourishment and protection. The God born on Christmas is bigger than human beings and knows that each and every organism is dependent on all of the others in an interconnected web of sickness and health. For *that* God of earth to be born in us is to make us acutely aware of how our actions impact the ruby-throated hummingbird and gray wolf and Alaskan salmon and killer whale and tropical rainforest and spotted salamander and osprey and echinacea and copperhead and tall grass prairie.

It is a terrifying and profound thing that such a God could be born in us. And it is an earnest prayer. For the hope of the future lies in just such a birth.

"Cast out our sin and enter in." We're accustomed to thinking of sin in a personally moralistic manner. But narrowing it to that is a red herring. What if, instead, we recognize how our complicity in factory farming, our obsession with plastics and all things disposable, our blindness to the simple needs of nonhuman creatures and contexts, our desire for material success and social acceptance compromise the well-being of beings today and yet to come? What if we recognize the perverse and damaging nature of those inclinations, then let the infant God of earth cast them out and take their place within us for comfort and joy and peace? What if *that* were the business of casting out sin and entering in?

Enough with the narrow-minded self-flagellation. Let's take a break from a navel-gazing sinfulness and look instead to what is bigger, what is more universally destructive, and begin there with the Christ child, divinity of blood, to guide us. "Be born in us today." I like that it's not only "me" for which I sing, where I ask that God to be born, but in "us." I'm only a simple, single person.

Oh, how I wish that the newborn God of earth, who comes with every concern of the planet for the whole dizzyingly complex earth, that the truth of a demanding sacredness in our fragile orb be born in/become clear to CEOs and hedge fund managers and contractors and army generals and so-called farmers who manage millions of acres from a high-rise in Manhattan. Please Jesus, God of earth, be born in them, too.

6

See Here, Wow

"With an eye made quiet by the power of harmony and the deep power of joy, we see into the life of things."
—William Wordsworth

Quarks, particles, black matter, and waves. What scientists are discovering about our universe borders on the mystical. Explanation demands language more akin to poetry than academic discourse. I imagine its practitioners wandering about in a wondering daze, for surely they pursue their work with as much sheer astounded-ness as did that biblical guy after Jesus put spit-mud-pie patches on his eyes or as Hildegard of Bingen in mystical transport. "In the end, finding out what's real may require redefining what we mean by reality," science writer K. C. Cole writes. "After all, science often requires that we go beyond sense impressions (as well as common sense)." She concludes that essay with a quote from Nobel laureate Steven Weinberg: "When we say that a thing is real, we are simply expressing a sort of respect."[1]

This enterprise, tracking the God of earth through the seasons of a church year, depends on such respect. For that matter, so do the Christian assumptions at its foundation. Is the God of earth real? Did God give to the world from God's self a *real*, redemptive incarnation? Addressing these questions requires thinking differently than in purely logical, concrete, and quantifiable ways. The Jesus story, what we have in and from the biblical narratives, demands consideration outside the confines of a linear history. Trying to make it conform to journalistic reporting is a frustrating exercise that ultimately flattens the story, dulls its edges, and makes us all argumentative.

Historians have good reason to question the geographical location of Jesus's birth, and few people disagree that Jesus's birth had to be in or before 4 BCE (not zero *anno domine*) for a number of reasons, not least of which is that the Herod who plays such a role in the narratives died in that year. The star that marked Jesus's birthplace from space is the subject of astronomical investigation and speculation; and whether or not winged angels from heaven regaled shepherds, who needed assurance in the face of such a shock, is a matter of interpretation or faith.

Nevertheless, we whose culture admirably champions critical thinking, replicable experiments, and evidence, evidence, evidence sometimes have a hard time accepting other kinds of truths. This is ironically most challenging for people of faith, some of whom fall down the rabbit hole of trying to prove what they believe. At work is the notion that if the details of Christmas are historically questionable, if they did not happen two thousand years ago in the ways that they're told today, then it's all a house of cards—Jesus, Mary, a God incarnate determined to repair relations with earth—all of it is bound to tumble with the first blasting breath of a question.

But there is something askew in the debate itself—wherever and whenever you think Jesus was born; whether Mary experienced a heavenly conception or was raped by a Roman soldier; if you are a Christian of any stripe or a disbeliever to the core. The quest to determine historicity, to ferret out and declare what *really* happened is all fine and good. But to yoke the truth to such investigation, to presume that what is real must be material or scientifically verifiable is another step and sometimes a misstep at that. Such an equation is not a given. Truth and fact are not necessarily the same thing. Fiction also traffics in the real.

The notion that earth, the nonhuman natural world all around us, under and even within us, could be an aspect of the redemptive incarnation of God is maybe not so much a function of external, material discovery like Lister and his moldy bread, but a recognition of the heart. The Jesus stories that take Christians through the seasons of the year are less a recital of history than a melody of the heart.

Human beings are storytelling creatures. Stories help us to understand our world, to find our place in it, and sometimes our purpose, too. So, the distinctions we draw between fact and fiction are rarely as absolute as we might wish them to be. Ask anyone. The truth lingers in Marvel Comics: "pow-wow," "shazzam," and all. Reality is on display in the struggle of Katniss Everdeen against a dehumanizing, mechanistic, and violently superficial world. The morals of a terminally ill person trying to secure his family's future just might indeed come undone. Stories "work" because at some point or somehow we find that they tell what we know is true.

The Bible is chock full of fictions that have become real in the ways that people have told and embraced them—not necessarily as a seven, twenty-four-hour day creation in some geographical location whence the biologically first *homo sapiens* were evicted; not necessarily that a Jewish girl went into labor after midnight on December 24 so that God could reconcile with earth. Cave, stable; Bethlehem, Nazareth; 4 BCE, some other time; "tomayto," "tomahto." All of the above. When the velveteen rabbit asks, "What is REAL?" the wise old horse answers that being real isn't an original or static condition. "It's something that happens." And it happens, he says, when you are really, truly loved. (An alternative title for Marjorie Williams's *The Velveteen Rabbit* is *How Toys become Real*.)

Look closely. The stories do not demand that we read them as journalistic reporting. Neither do they come to us as silly flights of fancy. That a universal and eternal God so desired amends with(in) earth that God would become a poor Middle Eastern baby in Roman-occupied Judea can be its own powerful truth. At the heart of it, the stories, well-loved, tell what is real. Were there angels? You bet. A "donkey, all shaggy and brown"? For sure. That little drummer boy and a crippled child, healed, who brought the baby his crutch? Of course. Or not. So what? For the tales neither digress into scientific explanations nor pontificate on the virtues of intellectual suspension. They simply invite us to listen and then they get on with the story.

If we step aside from the historicity argument and oh, star of wonder, appreciate instead the narratives with all their literary and theological dependencies, their historically bound contexts, discrepancies, simplicities, and sophisticated restraint, then we may find that it all becomes quite possibly real and true. And if in hearing the Christmas story yet again one stumbles on a bit of peace, of love and joy, the sense of God in earth, and someone to adore, then as for me, I'd have to say, every bit of it is true. And if it is true, in this deep meta manner, then perhaps the God of earth is just as real, just as true. That the God of all would choose to become incarnate in order to reconcile us to God hardly seems limitable. It could surely happen just as much in and of the nonhuman natural world today as in and of a boy-baby of two thousand years ago. Well, maybe.

To recognize holiness is a quality of wisdom. To see the earth anew as holy, capable of redemption and greatness is an awesome thing and, like the baby Jesus, can stir up problems, too. The traditional Jesus's "coming out," if you will, was marked by two quite different, at-large receptions. There was the reverent visit of the magi, aka the "Three Wise Men," on the one hand; and Herod the Great's determination to hunt down and kill the infant god, on the other.

What a study in contrasts. What a lesson in managing the holy. In their wisdom, the three kings from the East subjected themselves; in his fear, Herod sought to subdue and obliterate. We have the same choice, of course, in our relationship to the earth: whether to respect and honor its power and mystery, or to control its wildness/otherness to the point of its death.

I wish God would swoop in and correct our fossil fuel follies. But the God of earth does not manifest himself as the executive of a transnational alternative energy conglomerate any more than Jesus appeared as emperor of Rome with the world's power at his fingertips. What noise and exclamation accompanied Jesus's birth was witnessed only by shepherds in a field—only a few lowly folks out in the country. The world did not shift in any grand or decisive way. A few scrabbly locals came to witness and worship, earthy folks who had seen and heard the terrors of heaven announce joy and peace. Some shepherds came. It has the feeling of a comic farce.

How could the God of all possibly be interested in repairing the world from such an insignificant point? Even throwing herself on the mercy (so to speak) of the world, how could the God of all time and place possibly believe that the world would follow through in a manner anywhere close to satisfactory? This is a real question for me still.

Unless this is a spoof, some tongue-in-cheek demonstration of the idiocy and shortcomings of human beings, God must really believe that we can step up and keep our end of a bargain to manage the world responsibly and sustainably; God really believes that we are capable of being—male and female, image of God material—able to maintain order, beauty, and goodness, even to create and to exercise a dominion that honors the integrity of an elegant and sophisticated universe. God comes to earth not to wrest control and straighten it all out, the mess we've made. But God comes to earth as insignificant and vulnerable as a poor wee babe that barely anyone even knows exists.

There's a line of thinking among the faithful that it doesn't really matter what we do to the earth—drive ginormous over-sized trucks from McMansions in the suburbs with as many children as we can reproduce, to over-air-conditioned, multi-bedroom vacation homes perched on sand dunes along any given hurricane-track coast with moneys made who-cares-how and paving every inch of the way, *and God will fix it*. If what we do damages the planet, *God will fix it*, so this thinking goes.

The trouble is that the God of earth comes without fanfare and with no apparent ramifications. No one much notices. Only the locals and a few wise foreigners. It is a slow and relatively insignificant process of recognition. To state it bluntly: God ain't fixin' nothin' we won't fix ourselves. God isn't outside of earth like a master puppeteer orchestrating a course of action and effect that God so desires as to manipulate it into being. No, the God of earth has radically humbled God's self. We have to step up.

During these days by analogy with Christmas and Epiphany, the God of earth begins to be recognized more broadly, eliciting wonder, adoration, and worship from the wise—the ones who contemplate, study, and learn, question, and learn some more. And they bring tokens of wealth (gold), beauty (frankincense), power . . . and death (myrrh for anointing leaders and embalming corpses).

Today's magi can see within the mundane, the rude, and the dirty a shining presence of God. They may be as much exotic outsiders to religious or cultural expectation as were the Eastern potentates who sought the Jewish manger king. Yet though they may be from elsewhere, far away and different, these wise persons do not doubt. They recognize, through understanding the patterns of earth (its sky in the biblical magi's case), a potent sacredness among us.

But at the same time (cue the sound track of a dastardly villain), the paranoid ruler, the ostensible power of that place also recognizes the newborn God. And Herod sees the newborn not for promise and peace, but as a terrible danger to be killed as quickly as possible. Recognizing the God of earth means nothing less than an end to the world's business as usual. There is great promise—prosperity and peace—in such recognition, but the unwise powerful cannot see this and would rather kill all semblance of the holy than risk their bottom line. The significance of the God of earth complicates in inconvenient ways the business of some of the rich and powerful.

I say "some" because it's easy to think that only the poor and humble could understand and appreciate, even see, the infant God. Not so. The magi, whether they were kings or not, came with valuables that only the most wealthy would have had. They were powerful in their own right. Yet they also witnessed and recognized with deference and adoration the baby God. So today. Wealth and power do not preclude recognizing and honoring the God of earth.

Not all rich and powerful are the same. Here's how to tell the difference.

There are things that distinguish the magi from Herod in his wealth and power. One is wisdom. They are defined as magi—reverently studious, diligent in a learning that humbles even as it enriches mind and spirit. They attend to instruction and steward resources accordingly. So today, there are people and groups of people with clout and means who invest in the well-being of the planet with sophisticated understanding and a constant pursuit ever to improve that understanding.

Another way that the rich and powerful visitors from the East differed from the local power was that they gave. While the Herods of today seek to take—through an arrogant and selfish greed, life itself—the magi give. By analogy to the ancient magi, it's worth noting that one needn't know a particular religious tradition to recognize the God of earth, to seek to serve and to repair.

There is real hope in this, real hope that from quarters unknown and by parties with traditions unfamiliar to us, with different beliefs and practices might come fresh recognition and wise honoring of what it means for God to be of earth. And then there is grace. "The world is filled," Pierre Teilhard de Chardin writes, "and filled, with the Absolute. To see this is to be made free."[2] The magi brought stuff, but what they took away was more valuable still. "Beauty and grace," Annie Dillard writes, "are performed whether or not we will or sense them. The least we can do is try to be there."[3] Recognition is up to us.

PART III

The Glory of an Ordinary Earth

"Only miracles are simple; nature is a mystery"
—Robert Farrar Capon

For a long time, I found debates about miracles to be unsatisfying at best and usually uncomfortable, too. To take a miracle story "seriously," the choice was straightforward. Either you went with efforts to identify a scientific basis—the biological conditions that Egypt may have experienced to create a blood-like Nile to fit the exodus story, for example. Or if you were truly faithful, you'd simply declare that "with God all things are possible"—that God suspended natural laws to make the sun stand still or multiplied meager foodstuffs to feed a crowd (and with doggy bags to go). Neither approach works for me. Thank goodness there's another.

Albert Einstein, master of the real in the most calculably scientific of ways, is remembered as saying that there are "two ways to live your life. One is as though nothing is a miracle. The other is as though everything is a miracle."[1] Gravity as a definable force, how cliff swallows have grown shorter wings the better to dodge automobiles, that water is composed of air-type atoms, a farmer's immune system fighting off his melanoma, the social system of honeybees—each and every fact is nothing less than a blooming miracle.

"Ordinary Time" is the high-church term for the season that falls between the glories of Christmas and Epiphany and the ever-so-serious spirituality of Lent. Never mind that traditional Christianity maintains that the adult Jesus who walked and talked his way around Galilee and on down to Jerusalem was *God*. Yet this they call "Ordinary Time," as if there's nothing *extra*ordinary about it. And in truth, even in the face of Jesus's divinity, significant qualities of his time *are* pretty normal—he lived in a particular place, told stories, and made friends. Oh, and performed miracles. So, what does that mean in thinking about a Jesus beyond Jesus, about Jesus as God of earth?

7

Stories for Being

"Storytelling reveals meaning without committing the error of defining it."

—Hannah Arendt

With some time to kill, and why not a houseplant or two, I ambled the aisles of our neighborhood nursery for my next victim. Then I wandered outside. Rows of fruit trees stood in black plastic buckets beckoning for me to take them home. They had names like Red Haven, Goldrush, Belle of Georgia. And oh, the pictures on their tags were lovely. I resisted. We have cedar-apple rust, peach-borers, and deer, lots of deer. Then again, I reasoned, we also have a sizable garden surrounded by a seven-foot-high fence precisely to deter the local whitetails. I'd been looking for ways to cheat on the work such space demands. A tree would cut down the available acreage quite nicely.

And there it was: a glorious, shiny-leaved specimen covered by speckly, golf-ball sized orbs. Asian pear, the tag announced, self-fertile and resistant to the diseases that plague our region. I could almost taste the sweet flesh, feel that snap in my teeth and the juice on my tongue. I bought it on the spot. The first problem was my car—small, very small, even smaller than when I first drove up. Undeterred, I put the stately fellow's pot on the floor in the front, let the trunk angle between the seats, and lowered the rear window to give its branches the space they required. I hadn't noticed before how terribly windy it was. Gale force. Maybe better on the road? It was not better. The poor tree banged and whapped against the window frame. I drove faster. By the time I got it home, most all of the fruit that had been attached to branches exposed during our flight were long gone. Leaves were torn and ragged, the branches battered along the bark. And, of course, I hadn't prepared the spot.

Patience is surely a tree's virtue, however. It waited for me to dig an admittedly poor hole in even poorer soil, drop its root ball in, douse it well, and brush my hands of the whole business.

Wonder of wonders, it survived, and so well that the remaining fruit plumped and plumped as the weeks went on. In time, I thought, that fruit—all of it, and so much—would be mine. But the branches were young, slender, the fruit big and heavy, and I unwilling to cut off a single pear. The branches bent nearly to the ground. Finally, I harvested the fruit, and it was pretty good. Some rotted in the fridge, but we had a lot. The branches never straightened, however, and the next year, the tree didn't fruit at all.

"Oh," the nursery lady said, "some of them really do need another tree in order to set fruit." Another. It was too daunting. Besides, I felt so bad for how it had all gone down. The tree now looked pathetic and misshapen. But the year after that, this spring, I noticed its blooms conspiring with a long-winged, long-nosed wasp-type critter that I'd never seen before. And from the central trunk, the tree sprouted a shoot straight as a teetotaling sergeant that quickly overreached the others in height and girth. Those blossoms have now become tiny speckled orbs. If I've learned anything else, I'll reduce the fruits' number and treasure what remains. Grace abides, generosity, and mercy, too.

The biblical Jesus told stories, parables, by way of adjuring, instructing, chastising, and assuring. Of course he did. Jesus did much of his teaching by telling little stories such as the story of the Prodigal Son or the Good Samaritan. He used fictional people, circumstances, and places that were nevertheless familiar to Jesus's audience in order to get those who listened to think somehow differently. Stories are timelessly powerful ways to inform and influence. Frequently "made up," they nevertheless have the capacity to tell truths like no other. No outline of sophisticated argument or detailed report of factual events can hold a candle to a good story for visceral engagement of the sort that reorders the synapses of one's brain or the push and pull of one's heart. Who doesn't love a good story? Elie Wiesel says that God created human beings because God likes stories.

It would seem that the God of earth is telling stories all over the place. The Asian pear might just as well have thrown on a cardigan and made me a cup of tea before imparting its wisdom. I've heard geologists speak of "reading" rocks. Among the most magnificent is an epic: the Grand Canyon. It's a tale told in a complex, multifaceted series. Its pilot, at the canyon floor, even hints of a backstory deeper still. Each layer tells a moment in time and with a cast of characters fossilized in arrangements suggestive of mystery, drama, romance, and death. Of 70 million years its story tells.

Like the gospel parables, the stories of the God of earth could, I suppose, be read and even learned simply for entertainment. But there's always a point, a punch, a lesson, for those who would listen and attend. The snow atop Mount Kilimanjaro has been for so very long so consistently striking as to become iconic among the world's mountains. That snow is disappearing. There's a grove of aspen in Utah that is actually a single organism. Every one of its many "trees" actually derives from a single rhizome. Scientists estimate its age at between 80,000 and a million years. But Pando, they call it, is dying, and we're not sure why.[1] Monarch butterflies need milkweed, which grows wild in wide open spaces. But we have plowed those acres under for monoculture corn and are paving more and more for highways and shopping malls and suburban developments. Is it any wonder that the butterfly population has shrunk so drastically?[2]

Stories only work if people listen. What would it mean to listen to the earth's stories? Listening to the earth may be silently attending to the beetle in the leaves, the call of a frog for its mate, the dip and scoop of a pelican finding dinner in the waves. It may be watching how a bee burrows into the cucumber flower then the next and the next, or examining the rings in a fallen limb, or how moving water eddies around stones. Certainly, there's hard science involved. To listen well means attending to the learning of geology, microbiology, physics, and chemistry. But it may also mean leaning on the interpretations of poets, visual artists, and musicians to find and name the beauty that calls forth reverence.

Maybe it is simply bringing oneself into the presence of what is not self and laying the self bare there for whatever mystery may act upon it.

Jesus could have saved a lot of breath by saying that each person should care for others no matter how different they are or inconvenient the care instead of telling the whole parable of the Good Samaritan. But maybe he believed that there's something in the process of listening to a story with its particularities of detail, with its rhythm and style that has value, maybe even meaning, in itself. Or maybe the distillation is misleading. Maybe there's more to the story, more ways that it can mean, more depth and nuance than a single takeaway statement can capture.

And that brings us back to the stories of earth. There are thousands, millions, and more every day, every moment. They are what's happening all around us, if we would but have eyes to read and ears to hear. It takes work—a lifetime commitment to learning.

And it takes courage. It is an act of great bravery. To listen truly, with open heart and mind is to risk being changed. To attend to the stories of the God of earth demands that we put ourselves in a position—physical, mental, emotional—to listen.

A brief aside on each of those positions. First, a physical position might be as grand as the top of a mountain peak in some vast wilderness preserve. But it might just as well be standing before the fish tank in the dentist's office. It is to put oneself in a place to observe the nonhuman natural world. Second, we also have to be in a mental state suitable to listen. You don't have to have a Ph.D. in thermodynamics or decades of experience tending the elephants of an African preserve. But to cultivate a mental position to listen to the stories of the God of earth, one cannot resist learning the nuts and bolts of what we roughly call "science," and continue to learn this hard information (not difficult-hard, but solid-hard) throughout life. Meditation's not bad, either. Third, we need to be in an emotional position to catch the parable and examine it for ourselves. This may be the most difficult of all because it demands that we open up the most vulnerable part of ourselves. Sometimes that hurts.

The parable/lesson may be painful. It may incriminate, like Jesus's gift of the widow's mite. Or it may be painful because if you're emotionally positioned really to observe, to listen, you risk the devastation of empathy, of truly understanding the confusion and horror of a manatee cut up by a motorboat and starving because the Jet Skis have torn up all the sea grasses on which it once feasted. Really to listen to parables told by the God of earth requires an emotional openness that invites all kinds of feelings to the party, including the most uncomfortable—guilt in the face of our failings, solidarity with the suffering, or simply sadness in witnessing a world diminished in health and beauty.

But let me note another important quality of Jesus's parables: the quality of surprise. Reducing a story to some pithy take-home lesson also precludes this quality. And surprise is vitally important to the stories that Jesus told. His tales caught their audience off guard, dashed expectations, and sometimes unsettled with an unpredictable ending. If we're serious about this experiment, identifying the nonhuman natural world as Jesus, then we must be open to the stories that it tells catching us by surprise. One inevitable effect is a humbling: we can't presume to know exactly what the kingdom of God is like, no matter how well trained we are, how perfect our "positions"—physical, mental, emotional, spiritual. There's a pretty good chance it won't be exactly to our imagination or sometimes even liking. But if we are open, if we dare ourselves to watch/listen all the way through, I believe that the surprise (happy or not) will always be good.

Like the parables of the biblical Jesus, the parables told by the God of earth demonstrate a sophisticated system of interdependence in which we are called to do our part by right living, right work. But for all the clarity of earth's lessons and demands, the parables told by the God of earth are also full of surprise and wonder. And along the way, they shed light on and help us to understand the qualities of heaven and the ways and being of God.

8

Locating Home

"This is the place of places and it is here."

—Gertrude Stein

The God of earth, universal as this Jesus beyond Jesus must be, nevertheless is of a particular place. During this "Ordinary" season, the God of earth is home. By that I mean a few related things: rooted in and inhabiting a particular locale; in relationship to us by means of that place's unique nature; and (simply) *is* home—"where the heart is," as Pliny the Elder said; "the place where when you have to go there, they have to take you in," as Robert Frost said;[1] or whatever home is for you. The implications are profound.

"A certain Solomon here to see you." I had just arrived at the German Lutheran Youth Hostel in Jerusalem's Old City along with a dozen or so other students from St. Olaf College. A friend of mine back home who'd experienced the same semester abroad that I was undertaking had told me I should seek out this gregarious Palestinian shopkeeper. But he, Solomon, had beat me to it. Over the coming months, I spent many hours watching the world from the vantage point of a small stool just inside his shop door on David Street, one of the Old City's main arteries. It is a most cosmopolitan spot.

I was much less adept than Solomon and his friends at identifying the countries from which the tourists came—Germany and Japan, Korea and Australia, the Netherlands, Canada, El Salvador. But come they did, and from all over the world. Nearly all were Christians, and nearly all of them were eagerly retracing the footsteps of Jesus. For them, it was to walk where the God incarnate walked—an experience capable of enriching and enlivening their faith like no study or prayer or community experience could do. After all, the Christian Jesus, by definition, was of a place, an identifiable dot on the map.

Rather than hitching a ride on Ezekiel's wacky chariot, or dashing in and out of earthly space like the wrestling Jacob's angelic opponent, the traditional Jesus of this "ordinary" season hunkered down in his blood-and-bones life on a small wedge of territory just east of the eastern edge of the Mediterranean Sea. Christians go there today to feel a different kind of connection to their Savior than they can experience in any other way.

Place is part of our stories, of who we are and how we see the world. Inasmuch as we talk about the earth in a universal, global way, what we know of it are particular places: particular because of their unique natures, particular because of how they are to us, particular because each is in some way, to some one, home. Jesus is, according to Christianity, for all people everywhere. Yet, he was born, lived, and died in a particular place. That locale informed the imagery of his parables and how he was in the world. It was also where and how people met Jesus—a footwasher among dusty, sandal-wearing folk; a companion on rough water among subsistence fishermen; a problematic rabble-rouser who used mustard seeds and rocky ground and goats and a Roman coin to comfort the afflicted, confound the complacent, inject hope into despair, and generally challenge the powerful status quo. This, Christians believe, was the work of God incarnate as a human being living, working, loving, and dying in a particular place.

No different the God of earth. If a Jesus beyond Jesus can also be incarnate in earth itself, then we meet this God of earth in our own places, locations with which we are invited to develop a relationship that can be as exasperating and redemptive as Jesus was to his place. Given this concrete geography, our being in and of a real and specific place, the relationship is dynamic. It's a give-and-take with the God of earth that requires our attention to the particular places of our lives. Corresponding to the traditional Jesus, it is to share the space of the incarnate God—to learn from his wisdom, submit to her correction, and simply to marvel at the privilege of being in the company of God. It is also to be mindful in that relationship of others with whom we share the space.

Smaller houses, bigger homes.

Less material consumption in establishing and maintaining houses and a broader definition of the places we call home. In respectful relationship to our place, the God of earth can be present with comfort, instruction, and wisdom just as Christians recall Jesus being for the people of his time. But we have to come home.

I don't remember ever intentionally walking the whole of the stations of the cross, a popular route in Jerusalem, but I do remember threading my way through clumps of tourists, each holding a flag, wearing an orange beanie, or otherwise carefully distinguished group from group and guarding against disorientation in the maze of alleys and streets that thread through the Old City's four quarters. I remember weaving through, led by my sweet, sober Palestinian boyfriend to reach the arched doorway of his house, adjacent to one of those stations.

Guides explained the significance of the site, often in languages unfamiliar to me, as Issam unlocked the blue door and we slipped inside. He pulled the door shut behind us. At the house's center was a large courtyard, open to the sky. Even so, the cacophony from the street was barely audible. The ancient walls were thick and high. His mother brought tea, and I did homework while Issam drummed the taut hides of his favorite musical instrument. Meanwhile, outside, thousands of individuals had undertaken a spiritual exercise of connection to their God and Savior mediated by a particular spot on the far side of the family's living room wall.

Israel, like no other place that I've been, hosts a striking clash of interests and perspectives. Its natural, physical contrasts are at least as profound. Within a region smaller than New Jersey lie snow-capped mountains, sand beaches, lush vineyards, and rolling hills of barest desert. The Jordan River is a mere trickle in places, Galilee (more lake than sea) is quite shallow, and then there's the otherworldly landscape of the Dead Sea. It's different now, of course, than it was in Jesus's time. The flora and fauna have changed, not to mention the addition of modern trappings. Yet Christians still seek—and find—profound connection in Israel beneath their feet and before their eyes to the Jesus of two thousand years ago, who is alive to them as Lord and Savior.

The God of earth I seek must be, then, just as much about particular places as the traditional Jesus of Christianity. And just as that Jesus sought a relationship with the people of his hometown, of his home country, so the God of earth, despite his universality, is particular to the nonhuman natural places wherein we live. In and from those places, the God of earth calls us to listen; to hear the stories and take her lessons to heart. Jesus didn't bludgeon people with his message or forcibly demand an audience. Some accepted the invitation to relationship. Most did not.

Might not the God of earth extend the same invitation, offer instruction, promise redemption and life in its most full, if we would but agree to honor and respect the integrity of our particular place, the nonhuman natural landscape of *home*— our home—as the incarnation of God?

Wendell Berry, in writing of returning to his home in Port Royal after an extended absence, tells the nature of such relationship. "This place has become the form of my work, its discipline, in the same way the sonnet has been the form and discipline of the work of other poets: if it doesn't fit it's not true." The place is particular, special. But appreciating that is not enough. To accept the God of earth is to be in relationship. Only then, can one experience "the form of my work," what's alive, what's dynamic, what's true. "In the work is where my relation to this place comes alive," Berry writes. "The real knowledge survives in the work, not in the memory. To love this place and hold out for its meanings and keep its memories, without undertaking any of its work, would be to falsify it."[2]

Jesus's home was a particular geographical region demarcated by discrete boundaries, there on the eastern end of the Mediterranean. It was a "real" place, and people still go there— flying from Sao Paolo, Arkansas, Ontario, and Seoul. But because Christian tradition understands him to be the incarnation of an eternal God, the places where the biblical Jesus walked have a meta-nature to them. They did even then. It was where God had worked and over millennia had been urging people to join in. Because those Hebrews had accepted the relationship, Jesus and his followers already had evocative poetry situating the hope of the people in Bethlehem (Micah); Jerusalem was Mount Zion, the center of the world from whence instruction would go and people from all over the earth would come to learn peace (Isaiah); and Galilee abutted the Valley of Megiddo—Armageddon, where the cosmic apocalyptic battle of good and evil would finally be waged. The Jesus of Christian tradition was of a place even as he transcended sites defined by longitude and latitude to function as the center of the world.

Rather than advocating a course of land preservation, Barry Lopez urges us to think about recovery—but of a humble kind. He observes how human ideas of ownership over the nonhuman natural world have led us to expect performance and to punish the land when it failed to meet our expectations. For a long time, Lopez says, "we told the land what it meant. We weren't interested in any kind of conversation."[3] Why not a Jesus beyond Jesus, who meets us in our particular places, the unique and wonderful nonhuman natural land under and around each of us, and from there invites us into conversation, the same relationship of challenge and redemption?

And why not call that sacred place "home"?

Like a dove, the Gospels tell, God's Spirit descended on Jesus at his baptism by John, and a voice from heaven called Jesus, "My son, the beloved."[4] Blessedly unique, Christian tradition maintains, Jesus came to Earth as the one and only Son of God. Of all the planets in our solar system that scientists dating back to Babylonian and Egyptian astronomers have been able to identify, none compares to Earth.

I watched the movie *Interstellar* with some discomfort. Its premise supposes an imaginable future of such environmental devastation that Earth can no longer support life as we know it. The good guys seek a planet we might colonize, and it concludes (spoiler alert) with the discovery of just such a place. Wonderful. Not. The notion that we can ruin this planet and simply jet away to begin again is naive at best. But even if there were such a planet, and even if we could move there, that hardly excuses trashing this one.

"My beloved," the Earth, turns around and around out there in dark space, blue and green, whirling and spinning, aglow from the sun and swathed in night's shadows. "My delight," filled as it is with a dizzying array of life in all shapes and colors and sizes and melodies. Of God, and fragile as can be.

9

Friendship and All the Stuff of Earth

"We need another and a wiser and perhaps a more mystical concept of animals. . . . We patronize them for their incompleteness, for their tragic fate of having taken form so far below ourselves. And therein we err, and greatly err."
—Henry Beston

Miles of wooden boardwalk weave carefully from the road over marsh and sea-grass-covered dunes, past bogs chirping and "grr-oaking" with amphibians, skirting shore birds' nests and (hidden under the sand) the leathery eggs of sea turtles, who emerge perfect and tiny in their moonlit time and scramble to the salty ocean. Meandering along, one might see an alligator, flush an ibis, catch the scent of longleaf pines, and, when near the shore, will likely witness the peculiar grace of pelicans catching an updraft inches from the water's surface.

From the ocean's edge, looking back, that wild world is all one sees, with miles of sand so bright in either direction that one would have to squint to discern shells impossible to number. This isn't a pristine island far in the Pacific or a Caribbean hideaway. It's a U.S. Air Force base in Florida's Panhandle. An unlikely "friend," if ever there was one; but there it is. A staff of naturalists, people trained in forest management and wildlife preservation attend to this heavily protected spot. I'm told that's true at other military sites across the country.

This does not in any way absolve the American military of the guilt of its environmental devastation in manners and degrees right up there with the worst corporate offenders. But it does make any friendship with the God of earth even more striking. Tax collectors, men who betrayed their own people for personal gain, who fleeced honest folks already suffering under Roman rule were also included among Jesus's friends. Who, and how?

The traditional Jesus, Christianity's incarnate God, gathered friends to and around himself. The best known are his twelve disciples, of course. But others, too, provided companionship and even comfort in his years on earth. Still more people—across a demographic spectrum and socioeconomic range—followed and learned from the biblical Jesus. Mary Magdalene was so beloved a companion, noted in each of the Gospels, that people continue to wonder if she mightn't have been Jesus's wife. A different Mary, her sister Martha, and their brother Lazarus provided domestic companionship. The Pharisee Nicodemus consulted with Jesus and, after Jesus's death, helped to bury him. Joseph of Arimathea was a wealthy dude who gave Jesus his gravesite. Matthew, of the reviled tax collectors, became a bona fide disciple.

Jesus's friends weren't the calculated partnerships with opinion makers or masters of networking, solicited from among those who could make big things happen because of their resources or social connections. What made them candidates? They were around, and they were willing to join with Jesus, even though that meant joining with others unlike themselves. It was a mishmash community of some rich people, mostly poor people; some schooled in things of the mind, most simply skilled through experience at some form of life-providing work; some respected, most from among the overlooked masses, a few with despicable pasts.

They happened to be present, and they happened to see in the man from Galilee a teacher worth following, a person good to be around. The biblical Jesus gave much to friends— from food at a lakeshore picnic to health and healing. But Jesus also leaned on friends, accepted their help, their houses, their food. Jesus even asked for their strength and comfort. It may not have been even, but it wasn't one-sided, this friendship they shared.

The earth is not out there, a discrete entity in splendid isolation but enmeshed in all sorts of relationships just as Jesus was with family, friends, and disciples. The God of earth, like the biblical Jesus, is relational. The friendship works both ways. What makes a friend to the God of earth, to the Jesus beyond Jesus incarnate in the earth itself?

I began this chapter with a reminder of the intrinsic worth of animals, beings as deserving of respect as any human. Inasmuch as animals are part of the nonhuman natural world, of the God of earth in this book, we might also consider them friends of the God of earth. Consider Wendell Berry's wild ducks, the picture of domesticity and restraint; the bees whose busy work makes possible the fruit that we enjoy; even the vultures: what diseases might we suffer if they didn't clean the road kill we've left behind? Each wild thing abiding within the parameters of its home, taking what it needs and no more, behaving within the greater environmental processes as a part of, not separate from, the whole. And at their deaths, without fanfare or synthetic mediation, returning to and received completely by the earth.

So, animals surely qualify as friends of earth. Who among the humans? People such as John Muir and all those responsible for establishing and protecting our national parks must qualify, as do organizations such as the World Wildlife Fund, the Nature Conservancy, the Audubon Society, and many more.

In my region, I think of individuals who forgo the millions of dollars per acre they might get for selling to development companies and instead accept a modest tax abatement to preserve "open spaces" of lush rolling hills, forest and meadow, with breathtaking views of the Blue Ridge Mountains, springs, and countless wild-dependent critters. I think of my sister, Linnea, and her husband Jon, who hang their laundry outside to dry; drive hybrids at max 55 mph, if they drive at all; grow astonishing amounts of food in a backyard garden without chemical pesticides or fertilizers; and installed solar power in

their tiny Minneapolis bungalow. I think of colleges cooperat-
ing with local farmers and restaurants with kitchen gardens,
of Dr. Wangari Maathai planting trees across Kenya, and of
Chico Mendes who said, "At first I thought I was fighting to
save rubber trees, then I thought I was fighting to save the
Amazon rainforest. Now I realize I am fighting for humanity."[1] I'm delighted to report that I could go on and on. I'll bet
you can, too.

There's yet another shade of this friendship with the God
of earth by analogy to the traditional Jesus that I find to be a
kind of blessed absolution even in its chiding correction. When
visiting his friends Mary and Martha, Martha complained
to Jesus that she was doing all the work while Mary just sat
around enjoying Jesus's company and teachings. Jesus's gentle
chastisement was not of Mary but of Martha. I hear in that
encouragement to let go of fierce responsibility every now and
then and simply to listen, appreciate, to be revived, inspired, or
simply enjoy the nonhuman natural world.

Sometimes I get so preoccupied with washing and reusing
every plastic container that makes its way into our household
that I forget simply to savor the pot of beans perfectly done in
the company of happy dogs and wild birds. I neglect a walk in
the woods because I absolutely must integrate compost into
the heavy clay soil of our garden; or I don't appreciate the bank
of a hawk's wing as it rides invisible currents over the reservoir
at sunset in my haste to get back to the house and shut the
windows before the cold rushes in. Sometimes it's enough as
a disciple of the God of earth simply to let go of the practical
worries of business as usual and listen, watch and listen, to the
stories of earth.

There are times, this analogy with the traditional Jesus suggests, when the God of earth urges us simply to honor and to
take joy in this world, to shower its splendor with our attention, to spend what we have in celebration and reverence of its
fleeting wonders. Mary of Bethany often gets confused with
Mary Magdalene and both with the unnamed woman who
squanders precious ointment on the Jesus facing an imminent

death. It's a peculiar story in which again, Jesus chastises the conscientious. To those who in their responsibility argued that that ointment could better have been used to fund the needs of the poor, Jesus said, "She has done a good thing for me. For you'll have the poor with you always, but you will not always have me."[2]

The God of earth must then, surely, be urging us occasionally to set aside concern and responsibility, even our responsibility for earth itself, in order to enjoy the wonder and mystery before us. Say, taking time to visit a place soon to be flooded by a dam or wild animals before their habitat is destroyed.

There is value in the adoration.

That alone is admirable, memorable, even. Jesus said, "What she has done will be told in remembrance of her." We're reminded to honor and to take joy in this world, as it is, now. Maybe a woman with extraordinary scientific understanding "squanders" her training watching mountain gorillas rather than running laboratory experiments to find the cure for a human disease. Maybe the resident of rural West Virginia takes a break from fighting mountain top removal to hike to a mountain's peak and take in the view. Maybe they have chosen the better part.

By contrast, I'm haunted by a biblical story of tragic failure. The Gospels tell of a rich young man who wished to ensure eternal life.[3] He said that he already followed the ethical commandments. What was left to be done? Jesus's answer was three-part: to sell all he had, give it to the poor ("you will have treasure in heaven"), and "come, follow me." The man could not and went away downhearted.

I believe that most people are good. They work hard, take care of their families, are respectful and polite in their dealings with other people. Maybe they even visit people in the hospital, look after a neighbor's kids, bake a casserole for the grief-stricken, volunteer occasionally. Most people don't murder, cheat, or sleep around. At the least, they know when they've erred, and try to do better. I do not doubt that the people who invested in building the Keystone XL pipeline are "good

people." I'll bet that they love their children, do their best by
aging parents, try to remain faithful to their spouses, maybe
sit on the boards of hospitals or universities, try to learn about
political candidates and issues before voting, perhaps actively
practice their religious faith in places of worship. I believe that
most of us are pretty decent and upstanding in the day-to-
day. And then there's this: money (and convenience, status,
expectation).

Sometimes, I am that rich young man. Okay, maybe not
exactly rich—or young—and definitely not a man. But you get
my point. Friendship with the God of earth, the Jesus beyond
Jesus, prioritizes the well-being of a wonderfully complex world
over individualistic, short-term, material gain. So can we, who
are so decent and upstanding in so many respectable ways, give
up a bit of our material gain, status, convenience, and social
expectation to accept earth's invitation to "come, follow me"?

Can we adjust our thermostats to be slightly less "comfortable" yet more efficient? Can we spend a little more to buy
from a local farmer or a manufacturer-employer committed to
sustainable practices and decent wages? Can we support young
women who choose *not* to have more children? Can we elect to
leave beautiful places alone? Can we urge our government to
reward living near where one works, shops, entertains, social-
izes? Until we can effect the policy changes necessary to turn
some of these things around, can we decide to spend more for
responsibly produced and minimally packaged foods, for fewer
and better-made goods, for services that employ people rather
than machines or disposables (people washing dishes at institutions rather than more disposable containers and flatware),
for insulation rather than cheap fuel, tax breaks for renovating
rather than for new construction, investing in excellent public
transportation rather than more and bigger highways. And can
we recognize that in this giving up there is a getting back, that
in this, less is more and life explodes all around us and within
us? Sure, there's the eternal of the forever-and-ever variety.
And there is the eternal that is now. After all, all there is for us
is now. Right now, this moment.

There's promise in it, too. By analogy with the traditional Jesus, in the doing, there is life—eternal, even. And along the way, there's the privilege of companionship, of learning from and partaking in the presence of the God of earth. If friendship with the traditional Jesus is any model, then to "follow" the Jesus beyond Jesus, the God of earth, is to apprentice ourselves to natural ways, to learn again restraint and balance and joy, to take comfort in knowing our place within the great and complex web of things, to exercise our abilities in harmony with the needs and ways of the greater, nonhuman world around us, to appreciate beauty, and all in order—yes—that we might have life.

PART IV

In Solidarity with Earth on Trial

"Sometimes, Lord, one is tempted to say that if you wanted us to behave like the lilies of the field you might have given us an organization more like theirs."

—C. S. Lewis

There is a move afoot as of this writing to build a pipeline from Canada to Texas that would carry tar sands to oil processing plants. No one, not even its staunchest supporters, doubts that it is environmentally problematic. Some say it's a travesty. And no one claims that it wouldn't be terrifically expensive not only in infrastructure but also in the actual extraction process itself—spending fuel to get fuel. But arguments for job creation and oil independence are trotted out, the engine of powerful interested parties is strong, and let's admit it: it's exhausting to resist. Still.

Forty days, forty years, forty centuries. The Christian season of Lent recalls Jesus's forty days of wilderness fasting and temptation, which themselves recall the Israelites' forty years of wilderness wandering between Egypt and the Promised Land. These were periods of suffering, testing the mettle and honing the fitness of their subjects for greater, if different, trials to come. Recalling that, for Christians today, is a participatory thing—people "give up" stuff during Lent. But what does that mean in the context of the God of earth? What is the deprivation and trial of a Jesus beyond Jesus, incarnate in the earth itself, and how might people recognize that in their own lives? Two things: One, it tries the integrity of earth (like Jesus's forty days in the desert tested him). And two, we are compelled to dig down along with the suffering earth for a sustaining truth.

The earth, even as God's incarnation, suffers. It is subject to forces from weather to war, from farming to fire. We are the stuff of earth, limited and dying just as soon as we are born. But in our lives and in our deaths we are also part of something bigger than ourselves. Our solidarity with earth, with the God of earth, is as natural as our eating and breathing. So it is with the God of earth, even earth as the incarnation of what is eternal.

A sweetness laces the sobriety of the Ash Wednesday declaration that announces the beginning of Lent: "You are dust and to dust you shall return."

There is a time, the calendar tells, to deny ourselves—to deny ourselves the comfort and ease that an oil-dependent lifestyle provides, to eat less and closer to the bottom of the food chain, to choose water without plastic and wine from nearby, to walk. There is a season for solidarity with a suffering earth that may not solve earth's problems but just might solve some of our own.

So we dig down to discover our truth and accept our real nature, with all of its limitations. We close up our ears to the silver tongue that promises power, riches, and ease. Then, in embracing our fundamental vulnerability, even our weakness, we might just might find strength. Strength and the wisdom to resist.

The Gospels tell that Jesus fasted for forty days, and when he was tired and lonely and hungry, Satan came 'round. Three things the bad guy promised: bread, power, and riches. Each one Jesus rejected—not for itself but for how seizing them in such a way would amount to turning his back on God. When it was over and Jesus was alone again, "angels came and waited on him." Such is the season in which we find ourselves.

10

Dust, or When Holiness Wears Thin

"But I'll see you in the sky above,
In the tall grass
In the ones I love.
Yer gonna make me lonesome when you go."

—Bob Dylan

One of the reasons that I think young adult novels have such appeal to adults these days is not so much because today's adults never grew up. While that may be true in some cases, I suspect it's because what used to be specific to adolescence has leaked into adulthood, too: a quest for identity. Addressing if not answering the question, "Who am I?" is surely one of the most pressing, basic businesses of being human. As adults change jobs, dissolve marriages, move across the country or even the world, and have longer and longer lives in which to wrestle with the what, how, and why I am, stories of growth and the search for identity bear immediate and powerful meaning.

This season of trial and temptation begins by situating us. We take a moment in tracking the life of the God of earth to recall exactly who we are—an identity that, no matter what happens in between, is clearly defined at our beginning and again at our end. By analogy to the traditional Christian season of Lent and its launch with Ash Wednesday, we begin, and end, with dirt.

First, a brief retelling.

Once upon a time, there was nothing green or growing any-where. There were two reasons for this: God had not let down the rain, and there was no human being to take reverent care of the land. But when a spring bubbled water over the earth, the God of relationship and being fashioned a human from humus and face-to-face breathed it to life. God planted an orchard, beautiful and delicious, established the human being in it, and gave the him-and-her satisfying purpose: the human being would serve that place with reverent care, guarding its well-being, and in the process would live to human fullness in simultaneous relationship to earth and to God.

In time, things went otherwise, and terribly so. As a result, pain became familiar and impossible longing, too. What had been a blessed purpose became toil at which humans (divided now, into like-and-unlike, man and woman) would labor until each returned, dust to dust, back into the ground. It's a story of innocence lost, and of fractures busting along three seams, fractures deep and wide. It tells of a break between human beings (him and her); between human beings and God (and not just "God," but ironically the God of relationship and be-ing, Yahweh-God); and between human beings and the non-human natural world.

If it sounds familiar, yes, this is the second creation story in the Bible's opening book, Genesis. I don't believe the story's point is to tell of a once perfect time and place lost forever on account of human sin. I don't believe it has a single *point*, for that matter. But I do believe that there is something of it that still tells how we are in a complex world, and how we might seek and work to be, ever repairing those fractures in the face of knowing that we cannot, until in time we return, perfectly reconciled through and to the God of earth. Dust.

"You are dust, and to dust you shall return," the officiant intones over Christians recognizing Ash Wednesday. Here the traditional season begins. It's a curious bit of Scripture to invoke, fitting for the long march to the cross; but it also bears corrective and even, remarkably, a bit of comfort. The reminder of our dusty nature is almost always used in a sober, humbling sort of way. There's nothing particularly wrong with those associations. But they don't tell the whole story.

The relevant biblical texts, this from Genesis and another from Job, are much more complex and nuanced in ways immediately relevant for our thinking about the God of earth. They tell of an intimacy in relationship between us and the earth, of a respectful, even reverent partnership that promotes life and lends deep satisfaction and comfort. Those meanings disappear behind most English translations. Without a little explanation of the Hebrew, then, readers have no way to see the positive associations that a reminder of our dusty nature can bring.

The Bible's second story of creation, the Adam and Eve story in the garden of Eden, is the one that tells how Yahweh-God fashioned a human being from the humus of the earth. Unlike the previous story, narrated in Genesis chapter one, in which *adam* is created by the speech of a transcendent and disembodied God as male and female in the image of God, this second story tells of a God who walks around and makes stuff with God's hands. It focuses on a particular location. The narrator explains that the place was originally devoid of greenery because it lacked two fundamental things: water and *adam*.

Time out for a brief side note: *adam* is a biblical Hebrew word. It is not exclusively gender-specific, male, but can be translated as "human being," as well as "man," or as a name, "Adam." Hebrew does not distinguish between capital and lowercase letters, hence the diversity in translations of this story. Because the human being is not distinguished explicitly as "man" and "woman" until after God performs the surgery that makes of *adam* two beings, it seems best to translate *adam* at the story's beginning as a generic human.

When Yahweh-God fashions the human being out of the ground, it is as *adam* from *adamah*. There is a play on the Hebrew words for human being and the soil stuff of earth, related here, like the English "human" out of "humus." The story tells that God then planted a garden-orchard of plants defined by beauty and taste and put the human being into it.

After a detailed description of the place, the narrator repeats that God set the human being in the garden-orchard. But not exactly.

Again evident only in the original Hebrew, the narrator uses a different verb the second time around. The alternative verb suggests a way of placing the human in the garden that connotes comfort and satisfaction. It is the same word that Noah's mother plays on in naming him at his birth, a boy who will bring "relief, comfort." Especially striking is the context of the word. It is associated with the vocation of the human being, often translated "to till and to keep." This suggests, then, that the vocation of the human being in relation to the garden fulfills the person, gives a primary satisfaction, and is a comfort.

In other words, this is not grueling toil but a clarity of purpose and the satisfaction of doing it. The work itself, in the Hebrew, is hardly labor either. For the verb translated "to till" is a common one with a range of meaning: "to work, serve, worship." In other words, the story tells how the person's work is of reverent service to a land which is itself (explicitly described as) beautiful and delicious. Plus, that work not only defines the human (it is *adam*'s entire purpose) but also lends *adam* comfort, relief, and satisfaction.

That changes after Adam and Eve eat from the forbidden tree of knowledge; but it doesn't change completely. Their son Cain, in a poignant cry at the punishment he must bear after killing his brother, associates his experience of the presence of God with his relationship to land that he works. He is heartbroken at being torn from the land, which he equates (through sentence structure and the norms of Hebrew poetry) with the face of God. From the Hebrew: "you have banished me from the face of the soil. From your [God's] face I am hidden."[1] In other words, it was through the land that the first-ever child born not only knew God but also experienced the very presence of God. God of earth, indeed.

In the aftermath of disobedience, wherein the formerly fulfilling nature of *adam*'s vocation becomes fraught with difficulties (thistles and thorns), we read the Ash Wednesday phrase,

"For dust you are and to dust you shall return."[2] It's a different word, "dust," than the *adamah* from which *adam* was fashioned; but God equates them in this speech.

The other biblical text that Ash Wednesday recalls is from the end of the book of Job. That book wrestles with the nature of undeserved suffering as Job, a man declared absolutely righteous by none other than God, is nevertheless afflicted by all sorts of trouble. Speeches of Job and his friends constitute the bulk of the book as Job persists in maintaining that he is innocent and the friends try to exonerate God.

In the course of it, Job regularly requests that God explain, that God get involved in the discussion and argument to make sense of it all. But God is silent . . . until the end. When God does speak, it is not about Job's suffering or innocence or any of the arguments that the friends explored. It is all about the nonhuman natural world, and delivered in a way at once challenging and humbling. "Where were you," God asks, "when I laid the foundation of the earth?"[3] And God goes on with how God directed the details of creation—its architecture and order; the boundaries of a newborn sea, whom God swaddled with darkness; and a dawn that God commands each morning. We wait in vain for discussion of Job's plight, as God focuses instead on the constellations so grand and the eggs of ostriches, the gestation of mountain goats and the roaming places of the wild ass. On and on, in images great and small, but nothing of Job, nothing of human suffering. God peppers Job with questions, never for a moment entertaining the one that has preoccupied us through the entire book: How is it that bad things can happen to such good people?

Job's final response (and the last words he speaks in the book) is correspondingly odd-angled. It tells how differently he now sees and understands. Again, translation cannot do its multivalence justice. Job's brief speech is typically translated to conclude with a contrite Job saying, "I despise myself and repent in dust and ashes."[4] We can see why scores of readers conclude that he's simply been bullied into submission. But that is hardly the sum of it. The Hebrew words translated "despise" and "repent" are much richer than those English words allow, and in the context of the greater section beg alternatives.

The Hebrew word translated "despise" bears the meanings "to set aside, reject, refuse." The Hebrew word behind "repent" in this case can have the sense of "comfort" or "consolation," besides connoting apology. (It is a distinctly different verb than the one the prophets use frequently to urge the people to repent of wrongdoing and to change their ways.) In the context of extended speeches of God that have no apparent connection to the issue at hand—Job's innocence and terrible suffering—Job's declaration may express an aha moment like what is prized in Eastern philosophy.

That is, it's possible that God's speech functions like a Buddhist koan (designed to help the mind step aside from its logic-seeking enterprise to allow a whole new way of seeing and understanding). Job's declaration, then, may be one of enlightenment. His suffering is not gone. Neither does he have a straightforward answer to it or for it. However, suddenly the preoccupation with self, with justification and a cure for his ills, becomes irrelevant.

Job sets the self aside and realizes profound comfort in knowing exactly who and what he is: dust and ashes. Humbling, yes, but not defeatist. There is a paradox at work here: in setting the self aside, we may discover who we are at the most basic and fundamental—a discovery that is at once relief and consolation. We are of earth. Add to that the belief that God shared and shares in the experience of material being, with its attendant undeserved suffering. This is comfort indeed—to be of earth with the God of earth. This, the biblical stories tell, is who we are at the diamond-hard heart of it all—our identity at the beginning of time and again at the end of the day. Dust.

11

Hunger

"A complete fast is a complete and literal denial of self. It is the truest prayer."

—M.K. Gandhi

Why won't it just *rain*, I wonder, watching the sky, gray clouds tracking overhead, the soil cracking around the limp tomato plants. I've been dragging the hose through the garden, down the hill to the fruit trees, over to the magnolia, out to the new dogwood (itself a replacement for one I didn't water). But the clouds pass by, hoarding their droplets for who knows what or where, if ever? But these are the patterns, the rules of a complex ecology, and the earth won't break those laws, not even as it breaks in hunger and thirst.

A triad of temptations, that's what the Gospels say Satan threw at the famished Jesus: literal food, proof of God's presence and care, and power to own the world. Jesus's replies, issued on a faint head and rumbling stomach, were no, no, and no . . . not from you, and not on your terms. Concerning food, what we put into our mouths isn't all there is to life, Jesus said, but rather what comes out of the mouth of God. As for proof, Jesus's reply: Don't put God to the test. Of power and its terms (misplaced worship), only worship God, who is be-ing itself, and serve only that God. These were Jesus's answers.

In the face of mountains of plastic, polluted waterways, and climate change, some people say, stop fretting, the earth will fix it—maybe dramatically, maybe with a lot of death and destruction, but fix it at last to the earth's betterment. Hmm. This sure sounds like stones for bread. After all, it misses the point. The point is not some final, cosmic correction but our living up to responsibility for others in and through care for the nonhuman natural world today. Or there's the argument that God will fix it. If God really cares about the earth like that, such thinking goes, then don't worry; being all-powerful and all, He (always "He" in this argument) will fix it. But that sounds an awful lot like putting God to the test. Third, jacking up the use of synthetic fertilizers, herbicides, and pesticides on croplands to boost ever greater yields (never mind the poisoning side effects) sounds an awful lot like the devil's offer of power and privilege, if only Jesus would worship him.

Acts of God, insurance forms call them. Great big cataclysmic weather events—hailstorms, tornadoes, hurricanes, wildfire. I cannot blame the atheists and those ascribing to philosophies such as Buddhism or Confucianism for taking issue with the nomenclature, not least when personally subject to the destruction of such events, when standing in the rubble of what used to be the "family room" and now is an unfriendly pile of wires, soiled carpeting, broken glass, an upended La-Z-Boy, and nubbins of pink insulation.

It's hard not to take issue with the language (ascribing the trauma to an angry deity as our primitive ancestors may have done), when faced with modern science. Familiar with at least the basics—that multiplying greenhouse gasses while stripping ourselves of mitigating filters (trees, anyone?) is bound to cause imbalance, a "weirding" of the weather as much as (and related to) its general warming—the "God did it" explanation feels like a cop-out.

Or is it? In terms of the God of earth, the language becomes more interesting. Consider how it is that in the traditional story, Jesus suffered the same daily sorts of trouble that ordinary people did and do, and even more at the hands of other people. God did not swoop in to change that, despite Jesus's being also God, according to Christianity.

Environmentally traumatic events follow trauma to the environment. Our profligate use of fossil fuels has created the conditions for devastating weather events as painful to the nonhuman natural world (or more) as to us. The God of earth—the God who by divine choice became of earth itself in order that we might be saved—suffers without recourse to miraculous intervention but, according to the terms of earth, in order to give all, including us, a chance to be healed.

Hunger—the most concrete aspect of Lent—lends itself to all sorts of figurative connections; but during this period it is also simply and literally a basic need for food. It is traditional to fast during Lent. This has taken on some peculiar forms—giving up certain things, certain foods or drink among them; but it's also to eschew food altogether for discrete periods of time. Just as the traditional Lent invites some practice of self-deprivation in solidarity with Jesus's wilderness time, this season in the life of the God of earth invites us to identify with an earth who is enduring deprivation.

Religious people have for millennia used fasting to curb the pride and arrogance that comes with thinking that all accomplishments are our doing. For all our feelings of invincibility, or at least of strength and ability, hunger humbles. Getting anything done is not only much more difficult (if it's possible at all), but it also seems less important. Priorities shift around. Being still, in prayerful meditation, seems to be just the thing. Work is undertaken with new focus and determination. For one thing, it keeps the mind off food. But also, sometimes, the work becomes more selfless. It is work done for others, work done for God.

Hunger reminds us of our creatureliness. We are not our own, spontaneously derived from personal inclination and purpose. We are the product of a moment in our parents' lives, with or without their intent. We are earth-stuff of blood and bone. We slow down and fall over. We are carbon and mostly water. I'm always amazed when I read those statistics about how we are more water than we are anything else. The minority that is the rest holds us together and stands us up.

In its humbling chastisement, fasting recalls to us our dependence. We are dependent on the nonhuman natural world, and we are dependent on other people. We need food to live. Yet it comes from a world not of our making, and for most of us it passes through hands not our own before we eat. Deliberate fasting makes it easier to remember that we aren't so very great, independent, and all that. It makes it easier to marvel at the pleasure of food and a world that produces it in so many and varied ways. Going hungry, with religious purpose, awakens sympathy for creaturely others and gratitude for their part in feeding us.

Our abilities to be and do anything require that we be alive, and we must eat to live. But that's not enough, the biblical Jesus said. We get life at its most basic by listening and attending to what comes from the mouth of God. In the context of this book's experiment, that extends, then, to what earth is and has to tell us.

"The real secret of fasting," Robert Farrar Capon tells in his delightful hybrid of a book *The Supper of the Lamb*, is "that it is a mysterious way of lifting creation . . . a major entrance into the fasting, the agony, the passion by which the Incarnate Word restores all things to the goodness God finds in them."[1] Not bread alone; but from the mouth of God, restoration of deepest goodness.

To go without brings to mind another quality of this season: solitude. For all that hunger reminds of dependence, and for all the Lenten solidarity with Jesus in his wilderness time, the Gospels tell that the Spirit drove Jesus into the wilderness *alone*. His community didn't commune with him, his followers didn't follow. Concerning the God of earth, consider that sometimes it's best to leave the land alone.

"Thus far shall you come, and no farther." There is distinction between the sacred and the profane, say religious folks, and that distinction must be honored. Some things are simply off-limits to the majority, to the uninitiated, to anyone or anything of a certain category.

Jesus went into the wilderness alone. The God of earth, alone.

As Americans, inheritors of a crash-the-caste mentality, the we're-all-equals-here sensibility, we have an aversion to the forbidden, an inclination to "tear down this wall." This is often good, resulting in all sorts of levelings of what should have been level all along but got perverted by unjust hierarchies or prejudices. But. Some things are best left alone: God, sometimes, for example—hence the distinction between the sacred and the profane, the holy and secular.

In terms of the God of earth, it's worth considering that sometimes the best way to honor the nonhuman natural world is to leave it alone. Wild spaces are altered by our presence in them. I applaud the parks system, but I also wish that we weren't all so set on seeing a thing firsthand for ourselves but could rather appreciate it from a distance, a great distance even. Mount Everest is a trash heap, visitors report, littered with the refuse of the thousands of people with means and usually good intent who want to climb it. Our need to see the Arctic brings with it such fossil fuel demand that the arctic itself is disappearing for our very love of it.

If we consider the earth itself as Jesus, perhaps there are times and places to leave well enough alone, to let God have some God-time and space. Perhaps elect to see a photo, read a dispatch, be content with the imagination, and satisfied in the knowledge that at least by such a choice we're not making things worse. Besides, ask any two-year-old: there's wonder enough in our own backyards and right in front of our faces.

This season, this period of time is for reflection and repentance, according to Christian tradition. Why not think of that vis-à-vis the earth, in solidarity with its deprivations and in recognition of our part in them? That's what the season calls for, uncomfortable as it may be. But does the God of earth require that we hang our heads and flagellate ourselves for wrongdoing and harmful choices? No. A true fast, says the biblical God, is active and forward-looking. It is to "loose the bonds of injustice," to liberate, "to share your bread with the hungry," and to welcome as family at home those without such a place.[2] The beneficiaries of such a fast needn't be exclusively human, not in the least.

And in the end, after such effort, come the angels.

In the biblical narrative, angels swept in and finally ministered to the tried and tested Jesus. Even in earth's integrity, even with a suffering that is as predictable as it is severe, God is somehow present and at work in and through it all. There is succor and even aid that attends such honoring of the sacred and submission to what is holy.

PART V

A Crucified Earth

"I am at two with nature."

—Woody Allen

Among the most lethal forces of World War II was a tiny army, nonchalant about Hitler and unconcerned about sides. After wreaking a devastating havoc among troops and civilians alike, it found its ultimate foe in a solitary, nature-loving Swiss chemist. Paul Hermann Müller won the Nobel Prize in Physiology or Medicine in 1948 for discovering an insecticide that effectively controlled the spread of malaria and typhus. Americans soon found the compound to be agriculturally useful, too, and began a widespread spraying.

Forgive them, Lord, for they know not what they do.

When scientist Rachel Carson undertook to study the effects on the environment as well as human health of this wonder drug, dichlorodiphenyltrichloroethane, she discovered that among many species adversely affected (including humans) are predatory birds. The population of America's iconic bald eagle declined precipitously. Turns out, the compound, called DDT for short, caused fatal thinning of the birds' eggshells. In 1972, ten years after Carson published *Silent Spring,* the Environmental Protection Agency banned DDT.

In the face of now countless environmental abuses—human activity devastating to innocents of the nonhuman natural world for mere convenience or short-term gain—this story feels as quaint as Smokey Bear. Yet it reminds of several things. One is the high cost of hubris, the assumption that implementing some discovery favorable to a human purpose has no downside; and more to the point, that human need and purpose is distinct from the nonhuman natural world—that they bear no relation to each other. We couldn't be more wrong.

But another thing that this story recalls is how the thoughtful work of a few can set us straight again. Carson was no shrill alarmist but a hard-working scientist, who applied skills, resources, and attention to the problem at hand. But it took her work, the commitment of others devoted to making her findings public, and a public government willing to take seriously serious scientific discoveries. I am old enough to remember the rarity of a bald eagle, our worry at their careening toward extinction, and I'm grateful to those who took action.

Some years after the ban had taken affect, I remember a summer morning up north. I wriggled out of my sleeping bag before the sun, woke up my dad, and we rowed out onto the Canadian lake to fish for breakfast. I was still a bit groggy, I suppose, when a great whirring rush overhead so caught me by surprise that I nearly tipped us over. A bald eagle—heavy and huge—had taken off from a bare pine nearby. We watched as it rose over the water, cleared a far island, and disappeared. When the sky brightened we lifted the anchor. Overhead, with the "*whoomph whoomph whoomph*" of strong wings in flight, the eagle returned.

This brief biography of DDT finally also reminds us that there is hope for renewal, forgiveness, and life. This is the hope carried by Christians through a somber mini season of the church year known as the Paschal Triduum (a term I can pronounce no better than the long form for DDT). Beginning with the celebration of the Last Supper on Maundy Thursday and continuing through Good Friday and Holy Saturday to Easter Sunday, this period recalls Jesus's mandate to remember his suffering, death, and resurrection. Some say it's the whole Christian point of Jesus, the moment when Jesus finally and absolutely healed the rift between us and God, effecting a forgiveness that absolves as it heals.

And what of the God of earth? Can we who witness its crucifixion, who grieve its death and mourn its loss, also find renewal, and through a newly vibrant earth gain the wholeness of redemption?

It all begins with dinner.

12

At Earth's Table

"There is nothing to eat,
seek it where you will,
but of the body of the Lord."

—William Carlos Williams

I love that we have to eat. No choice about it. We must have food in order to live, and I do so love to eat. There is no more intimate connection between us and the nonhuman natural world than food. Eating is both unavoidable and un-proscribed. There is no alternative, no whether-or-not to eating, and we lucky few have countless choices of what and how to do it.

This moment in the year of the God of earth is analogous to the Last Supper, that spring evening in Jerusalem when Jesus said, "Everyone who wants to be in the picture, get on this side of the table." Okay, no. The speech that *is* remembered, the words that Jesus spoke over the meal before them, institutes a crucial ritual for Christian tradition—"the Eucharist," "Communion," or "the Lord's Supper." Although those "words of institution" vary depending on the Gospel and denomination, there are three commonalities: bread and wine; the charge to remember; and that it's "for you," usually spelled out as the forgiveness of sins.

What does it mean, then, for us to approach the earth's table as an altar, to "remember" the God of earth in receiving with reverence her body and blood, and to recognize that something in that sanctified process is restorative, even redemptive?

There's the food, of course. Perhaps the poet says it best, like William Carlos Williams. But scientists can be poets, too. "If you wish to make an apple pie truly from scratch," Carl Sagan said, "you must first invent the universe."[1] We all know the stats: by eating lower on the food chain, choosing things raised responsibly and sourced close to home, and preparing them with a minimum of energy, we reduce our carbon footprint, minimize the suffering of others, and even possibly gain personal health along the way. But considering the earth as a Jesus beyond Jesus gives those choices new meaning. After all, the table is not only about food. It's also about manners.

Like many fans of Wendell Berry, I have loved his poem, "The Peace of Wild Things." So I was delighted some time ago to have an opportunity to hear him read it aloud, in person. The context was an interview conducted by Duke professor of theology, ecology, and rural life, Norman Wirzba in the company of a large gathering of religious and biblical studies folks. Eliciting a collective sigh of approval and anticipation, Dr. Wirzba asked if Mr. Berry would read that poem aloud. He did. It concludes by observing the ways of waterfowl populating a nearby pond—how their wildness can be a solace to the human being beset by worry and care. When he finished, gentle "mmms" floated through the air like a subdued white-people version of a black congregation's call and response. Then, Mr. Berry shattered it.

He said he didn't approve of the poem anymore and now thinks he had it all wrong, that it's problematic and misleading. In the pained silence of that gathering after Mr. Berry had dropped his bomb, he said that what was wrong was this: the birds are not wild. They were and are the picture of domesticity and order. They know their place and are respectful of living within the limits of a natural balance. It is we, Berry said, who are the wild ones. We run rampant, without control or restraint, attending only to ourselves and our individual wants with no regard for our greater place in time and space. I don't have his words exactly right. But that's the sense of it. And in the face of urban sprawl and drill rigs, McMansions and factory farms, it's good sense. We have lost our manners.

I'm not sure which etiquette maven first said it, but I remember hearing that the first rule of good manners is to make others comfortable. The apostle Paul had a Miss Manners moment in Corinth. Apparently, Jesus's followers observing the Lord's Supper after his death had gotten out of hand with it, and the result was imbalance, alienation, and distrust. The meals had devolved into hierarchical systems and general misbehavior. Neither of these, Paul maintained, were what Jesus had in mind when he charged his disciples in that Upper Room with carrying on the supper practice. In truth, he said, eating like that was no Lord's Supper.[2] A true Eucharist has posture. No slouching free-for-all, it requires discernment—recognizing the body of Jesus in the food and the drink, with all that that means.

Surely Paul's correction and advice apply to the earth's table, too. The discernment and the manners go hand in hand. If we who have so much might whittle back every so often (or always) to moderate our consumption, then everybody (ultimately the whole planet) will feel more comfortable. If we ate lower on the food chain, for instance, and a bit less, if we chose foods with little or no packaging, that hadn't depended on vast systems of transportation and storage, which themselves depend on nonrenewable resources whose consumption is inevitably damaging (big breath here), then more of us—human and otherwise—could also live, and actually live in ways that honor the earth. "The justice of eating," Pablo Neruda calls it.[3]

The meal that is a remembrance of the God of earth—sustaining, sacrificing, and redeeming—is a community affair, whether or not we happen to be eating alone. The traditional "Lord's Supper" is also sometimes called "Communion." That communion has two interlocking sides. Communion with Jesus is one. It happens, traditionally through the active ingestion of what Christians in various levels of literalism consider the physical presence of the incarnation of God—Jesus's body and blood. The second is communion with others, sharing the moment of food and drink with other Christians, during which time their relationship to each other is recognized and affirmed. At earth's table, discerning within it the God of earth, we are buoyed by the presence of a God who chose to be of earth, with us to teach and to heal. We also share in the community of all those who inhabit the earth with such a posture of reverence and grace.

This is the Lord's table. This is the earth's table. Remembering the God of earth, all of us share in the body of God. We share in the earth, on the earth, together as one people, including the nonhuman members who live in their own integrity with balance and respect.

Yet none of us is without flaw, any less than were the disciples who gathered with Jesus at the Last Supper or the Christians who have over the centuries followed. Hence what's to come as the season's time ticks on.

Sometimes our eating is bloody and brutal, profane. We forget, and bypass the table of the God of earth for a thoughtless drive-through snack. We all transgress in our different ways. "I am a frayed and nibbled survivor in a fallen world . . ." Annie Dillard writes, "I am aging and eaten and have done my share of eating too." But there is space, even in such a state, Dillard notes, to stand in awe and affection before the earth that we share, "whose gnawed trees breathe a delicate air, whose bloodied and scarred creatures are my dearest companions, and whose beauty beats and shines . . . under the wind-rent clouds, upstream and down."[4]

The Jesus beyond Jesus, the God of earth, asks remembrance: "Think of me." When we do, when we are thoughtful about it, a lot can happen. Among the first is simply gratitude. How can one not say thanks, and not just speak it but gape in wonder in delight at the God of earth's great generosity? "You don't just say grace," Peter Mayer sings, "before you dig in. You stand and dance and sway around the kitchen. And feast your eyes astounded by what you've been given."[5]

When I visit churches that happen to be celebrating Communion, I inevitably get choked up. I find it awfully moving—the whole thing. It's an odd bit in the service. In an otherwise orderly, orchestrated system centralized by the gown-bedecked person(s) up front, during Communion, things break down. Only the giving-of-the-peace moment, when attention scatters throughout the sanctuary, compares, and that only barely. A kind of anarchy takes over. There isn't only one tested and qualified party running the show but lay volunteers—preoccupied, sometimes nervous—or a gaggle of self-conscious high school kids, perhaps a family—preteen on up—directing people in the pews to come forward, one pew, one line at a time.

The lines are never even. Plus, there are always some people who elect not "to go up," so there's the awkward shuffle around them in the pew. And then there's the partaking itself—to dip or sip? The wafer that sticks to the roof of one's mouth or the bread torn so generously that one works it for some time after leaving the altar, feeling for all the world as a novice to the whole bread-eating enterprise. There's silence, and there's music—the thin threads of voices carrying on while the choir is at the altar, people praying and other people looking around.

It's all quite beautiful.

What really gets me is how we're all in this together—the lumber of the man with Down syndrome, holding his ancient mother's hand with the same innocent need as the little girl walking behind him in baggy purple tights and a sparkly tutu, clinging to her dad. There's the well-dressed captain of industry with his country club family, and the congregation's newest member—divorced, they say, and looking nervous, new to town, too. There's the thirteen-year-old on crutches and the elderly couple who look more like each other than like anyone else here. All of these individuals, each one with her or his concerns and joys, insufferable tics, and surprising talents. How much more poignant the meal that recognizes and remembers the God of earth, gracious in her generosity, welcoming with Earth's own body the world, even including his betrayers, to the feast.

13

Principalities, Passion, and Power

Then, I fell in love. For years, decades even, I'd worked to establish an easy-on-the-planet lifestyle. Finally, I didn't need to drive for much of anything but walked instead. I grew a lot of what I ate in a tiny backyard garden, and my job was carbon neutral at the least—reading, writing, and teaching. But as soon as my heart went pitter-pat, I threw it all out the window. I roared back and forth by airplane and automobile to spend time with my boyfriend several large states away.

I wish I could say that it was an aberration in an otherwise environmentally flawless life. It's not, but only one of countless examples of how quickly I've forfeited my "principles" to some selfish end or another. I still do it, still make moral compromises all over the place. "Could you not stay awake with me one hour?" the beleaguered Jesus, on the eve of his arrest, begs his disciples. They could not. Then Peter, most vociferous in protesting that he would never deny Jesus, does deny him, three times, lickety-split, before it's over. Jesus's own community, in the power of its institutions, stood not against the power of his time but instead with it, with Rome, and cried out for his crucifixion.

With the God of earth on trial, even those who have learned at its feet and supped from its cup, turn away. Not only that, but we outright betray. "Nature lovers" come by the millions, but few are willing consistently to make loving choices. But there's more to the trial than where one's sympathies lie. By analogy to the traditional Jesus story, there's much more at stake even than personal integrity. What the God of earth requires is a willingness to upend our dearest, most deep, and profound beliefs. For the Sanhedrin, Jesus's claim to be the Messiah, the Son of God, was an intolerable blasphemy.

The experiment of this book asks what happens when we consider the Christian Jesus to include, to be, the earth itself. So, what happens when the God of earth stands before the powers of the world with a claim to be coexistent with what is sacred, what is life? What happens when the God of earth promises a richer life than riches themselves? We can't stand it. Among the religious, it is blasphemy exactly the same as the Sanhedrin deemed Jesus's claim to be. By such "nature worship," we forfeit the faith of "Jesus is Lord," and "only Jesus" that many Christians espouse (based as it is on interpretation of tradition and Scripture).

Among those whose touchstone of purpose and meaning is material success, to claim that growing the economy may be shrinking our lives is downright heretical. "If a man walks in the woods for love of them half of each day," Thoreau wrote, "he is in danger of being regarded as a loafer. But if he spends his days as a speculator, shearing off those woods and making the earth bald before her time, he is deemed an industrious and enterprising citizen." It needn't be this way, but until very recently, many Christian institutions were loath to participate in the environmental movement lest they be seen as nature worshipers.

Finally, it's up to the political powerhouse of the day to make the call. For the traditional Jesus, that meant Rome. But Rome, with Pontius Pilate as its proxy, simply threw it back on the people. So, too, for the God of earth. Only when the governments of the most powerful nations in the world establish a price for carbon commensurate with its capacity for harm can we arrest the environmental crisis toward which we're careening. But the nations won't do it without us. The God of earth stands on trial. Pilate hands it back to us. And with every drop of cheap oil, we cry, "Crucify him!"

"Purity," Teilhard de Chardin says, "does not lie in separation from but in deeper penetration into the universe." The God of earth, like Jesus, goes to the cross without theatrics or miracles, without supernatural rescue of any kind, but bowing to the terms of life and the natural laws of our planet. There, Earth abandoned in its agony cries out, "Why have you forsaken me?" Silence. God issues no answer. There is no spiriting away, no supernatural erasure of the awful events leading up this travesty, no miracle. Just the pain. And the death.

For a month, the *National Geographic* lay face down on our table. I couldn't look, didn't need to see to know: elephants cruelly brutalized, their tusks amputated to feed a vibrant ivory trade. You've seen the images—sharks for their fins, gorillas for their hands. I suspect that like me, you wish you hadn't and never would again. Shore birds struggle against the oil that coats every feather, polar bears slowly starve for lack of ice for hunting, monarch butterflies perish in the endless miles of Midwest monoculture, hatchling sea turtles cannot find the ocean for the light from high rises that line the coast.

I remember driving out West, some years ago. The foothills gradually yielded to ever more magnificent mountains, and then we came around a bend and saw something new. My dad's head. That's what I thought. It was shocking—a mountain so shorn that it looked bald. But what looks good on my dad does not look good on a mountain. A worse shock greeted me recently in West Virginia, where our hunger for coal has actually beheaded the mountains themselves. Seeing this the first time was like an odd trompe l'oeil: the top of a mountain obscured by mist, by clouds. But it was a clear day. The top was simply . . . gone.

I don't want to look. I don't want to see. How the followers of Jesus could stand to witness his crucifixion, I'll never understand. But they did. Each of the Gospels tells that at least some of his people were there. It was women, mostly women. And women who afterward attended to the corpse. It is the poorest, ironically the ones who have contributed least, if at all, to our environmental crisis who are forced to watch, who suffer the worst. There are all the innocent nonhuman beings, of course. But it's true for us humans, too.

With a handful of students, Bill McKibben spearheaded an initiative known simply as 350. After scientists discovered that that is the number of molecules of CO_2 in parts per million that our atmosphere can manage and still sustain a balanced life on our planet, McKibben's crew organized a global effort to seek to bring our existing number, far in excess (presently at 400 ppm), back down and to hold it there. On October 24, 2009, millions of people demonstrated their support, actions poignantly captured in images relayed from around the world.[1]

Among the initiative's goals is reaching world leaders to change national policies. At the subsequent Copenhagen conference, 117 nations signed on. The trouble, McKibben noted, was that they were precisely the nations with little or no resources or clout, already producing a fraction of the world's CO_2. Wealthier nations made of the gathering little more than "a charade," as McKibben called it.[2] It doesn't have to be that way.

A rich man, Joseph of Arimathea, secured Jesus's dead body and gave up his own tomb for a place to bury Jesus. Culpable or not in the death of the God of earth, there are those among today's wealthy who revere the planet, lend resources for its respect, and mourn its demise.

I want to say one more thing about this death—the death of Jesus and the analogous death of the God of earth: Fear. It lay at the foundation of that ancient crucifixion, and it hunkers at the base of our failures today. Fear like a virus grew and spread among the powerful until with their power they destroyed the Son of God. Among the Romans, the fear was of a sort concerned with stability and order within a volatile population in a tinderbox season—Passover. Fear within the ancient Jewish establishment (not the Jews as a whole—Jesus's own followers were Jewish, as was he) was of a religious sort. Such a person, a *human being*, could not claim to be coexistent with the eternal Creator God and go uncorrected. Fear within the powerful leads to devastating things. I submit that we face analogous fears with respect to the God of earth.

Nations and their governments are terrified to take the kind of action necessary to arrest an environmental crisis. They are terrified that it will bring economies crashing down and with them unprecedented social unrest. On the mundane level, they're terrified they won't be reelected. And then there's this: the nonhuman natural world is wildly complex. Honoring that opens us up to the horror of having to share—having to share space with wild things, water with future generations, and resources—well, we need to figure out how to think about such things as trees and minerals and soil differently. It means allowing others to live, sometimes to our own detriment— snakes, spiders, insects of all kinds. And we have forgotten how to live with such others. We are afraid of them.

Some years ago, a friend stayed at my house while I was out of town. She was from Poland and had been studying in Spain. The American South was new to her. Over the phone, she told me in a sweet, calm voice that "a small creature, very quiet and gray" had taken up in my pantry. "It doesn't move," she said. "It's very shy."

A cat door led in straight from outside to the pantry, and I had my suspicions. "Does it have a long tail, pink, without any fur?" Yes, she said. I explained that in our part of the world we have a saying, "playing 'possum." We talked a little about how she could manage it, to include leaving it there until I got home. But she fetched a leather glove, carefully lifted it by the tail, walked it out the back door, and set it down. She told me that it scampered under the wide deck.

I arrived home the next day and was working in my office when an uproar from next door drew me outside. "Kill! Kill! Kill!" the youngest of my former neighbors' three kids yelled while his father screamed to his wife to get a shovel. "It could have rabies!" the mother shouted, when I asked them to leave it alone. They refused to hear that a rabid animal wouldn't be afraid. To the thrill of the children, the man beat the opossum to death.

Fear is part of the problem—of individual animals like the opossum but also of what is wild, what is latent in the power of the nonhuman natural world. Motivated by fear or by greed, ignorance, laziness, or some combination thereof, we are all complicit to some degree or another in the planet's woes.

But let me be clear here: if you already care at all, if you are trying to live responsibly on the planet, then you and I, dear reader, are hardly the ones pounding the nails. So, if we spend our time attacking each other, already acting with eco-logical sensitivity, then we have let Rome—the greater world powers—load onto us their far graver sins. Which brings me to Saturday.

14

Grief

"Since the 1990s, the number of Monarch butterflies has decreased an incredible 95%, due in large part to the destruction of its main breeding habitat in the Midwestern Corn Belt. Monarch butterflies exclusively lay their eggs on milkweed, and their caterpillars rely on the plant as their only food source. But due to unchecked spraying of highly toxic herbicides manufactured by Monsanto and Dow on genetically engineered crops, milkweed plants have been nearly eradicated in the monarch's key habitat. By some estimates, monarchs have lost 165 million acres of habitat, an area nearly the size of Texas."
—from a petition begun by Maine congresswoman
Chellie Pingree, February 2015

So it happens that a weeping sadness and fist-flinging anger get all tangled up in the lines of grief.

In rural Minnesota, once a year, a tiny Swedish Lutheran college (alma mater of my mother, my grandmother, and my great-grandmother) hosts its annual "Nobel Conference." Prize winners and other extraordinary thinkers from around the world convene at Gustavus Adolphus College to discuss publicly a particular theme. At the forty-eighth such gathering in 2012, Kathleen Dean Moore observed, "It may be one of the biggest triumphs of big oil . . . to make consumers blame themselves for climate change even while they're spending millions and millions of dollars to make us mindless consumers . . . while they do everything they can to make sure that we don't have alternative ways to travel, alternative jobs, that we don't have alternative ways to heat our homes, alternative ways to ease our grief."[1]

She was angry. I am, too.

The women at the foot of the cross did not crucify Jesus. The disciples, though they may have denied and even betrayed him, did not crucify Jesus. The authorities, religious and political, crucified him. Among Elisabeth Kübler-Ross's stages of grief, anger may be the most common, most consistent. "Yes," Moore said with that conference audience, "Yes, I need to reduce my use of fossil fuels absolutely dramatically. Yes . . . but *I* didn't cut corners and cause the oil gusher in the Gulf of Mexico, and *I* didn't do my best to undermine the EPA and every other agency that might have controlled fracking under farms, and *I'm* not lobbying Congress to open oil drilling in the Arctic Ocean, and *I* didn't cut funding for alternative energy sources. . . . I am not going to let those people whose business plan is to wreck the world offload their moral responsibility onto me and disempower me from acting."[2]

Anger it is, but inseparable from sadness. I had the opportunity to hear Dr. Moore speak at a different conference in Seattle. It was a conference of writers, and Moore's panel concerned the work of writing for social change—for justice and peace, environmental and otherwise. Two things in particular struck me then and have stayed with me ever since. One was her reply to a participant's complaint that their readers are probably already on board with whatever is the issue at stake. "Aren't we just preaching to the choir?" the person asked. "Maybe so," Moore said. "But the choir is tired." Whatever might help buoy us in the work, lend comfort, inspiration, levity is surely worthwhile. "Plus," she added, "If you've spent any time in a choir, you know that not everyone is always as righteous as they may like you to think."

That got some laughs. What moved me to tears was related to that tired choir: Moore's recognition of grief. Anyone who cares, anyone who is paying attention cannot help but be deeply and profoundly sad. Yet, Moore observed, we are not allowed to reveal such grief. It's a downer, a buzzkill, and frankly useless, this mourning the loss of species, this horror at the rippling effects of melting ice caps, this terrible sadness in the face of family farms paved under and rain forests denuded. To respond with such naked emotion; no, grief is not allowed. Yet in the face of such deaths, how can we who loved the crucified God of earth not but?

In the year of the God of earth, like Holy Saturday, the day between Jesus's death and his resurrection, there is time for grief. "The world to-day [sic] is sick to its thin blood for lack of elemental things, for fire before the hands, for water welling from the earth, for air, for the dear earth itself underfoot," Henry Beston wrote.

Grief is a survivor's business, and it *is* emotional. Grief isn't practical. It doesn't change anything, correct wrongs, or otherwise repair what is broken. But its expression undertakes important work. Grief honors what is lost, the life now gone, with a respect that acknowledges the effect of that life. Each of the Gospels notes how a wealthy man appealed to the Romans for control of Jesus's corpse. When Joseph of Arimathea had secured Jesus's body, he laid it in the tomb that this Joseph had purchased for his own body's burial. His actions didn't *do* anything to correct the assassination any more than did the women's tending with cloths, perfumes, and ointments, as the Gospels all tell. Yet such care surely honored the dead Jesus in keeping with their relationship to Jesus in life.

Another aspect of grief acknowledged is how it can ease the grief of others. Like the burden of a coffin hoisted on the shoulders of six pallbearers, grief shared is lighter. What may have seemed unbearable becomes manageable or at least endurable. For surely the most tragic possible effect of grief is suicide, when the survivor cannot finally survive. In the face of the death of the God of earth, then, we are compelled to sing "the brokenhearted hallelujah," as Dr. Moore borrowing from Leonard Cohen encourages. So, throats aching with grief, we sing.

15

Was There Compost in the Garden of Eden?

"If you don't have available space because you have filled every corner of your yard with priceless perennials, take out some priceless perennials. A compost heap is that important."
—Nancy R. Hugo

Ask any gardener. The single most important ingredient for success, for a bounty of growth and beauty is . . . drumroll, please . . . death. Somewhere on the property of any self-respecting grower is a gangly mass of brown leaves, carrot peelings, eggshells, and poop. Compost. It's the magic bullet, the humble savior of life at its most basic level, the soil. Was there compost in the Garden of Eden? Of all the koans I've invented, this is my favorite. Okay, it's the only one. It's a puzzler, all right. The Garden of Eden is touted by the biblically minded as glorious in part because there was no death in it. Yet its primary identity is as a place of plants beautiful and delicious. How to reconcile the two?

To make the perfect compost, www.almanac.com offers a video with commentary. "There are four ingredients," the narrator says, "Greens, browns, air, and moisture." At issue, I learn, is the ratio of carbon to nitrogen, which already makes me doubt I can pull it off. Ratios below 30:1 are "greens," he explains; higher are called "browns." Ai yai yai. The perfect compost pile will have two to three times more browns than greens, plenty of air (provided by turning loosely), and is "moist but not soggy." Phew.

You may do it like that, and I'll bet it's great. But if it sounds too daunting, simply do as most of the rest of us do: pile up old leaves, add kitchen waste as you have it (and the poop of herbivores if, lucky you, you have it), maybe mix every so often, and wait. Eventually, by some natural sleight of hand, that pile becomes crumbly, rich compost.

Death is not always the enemy. Jesus's death according to Christian tradition was both the doing of the sin of the world and a necessary act, an act that had the power to absolve human beings of their sin and so to repair our relationship to God. And for the God of earth? As uncomfortable as I am suggesting that its death is necessary, the analogy must be explored.

Any human activity that undermines the well-being of earth, that subjects the nonhuman natural world to death is surely as sinful as any traditionally moral infraction. In his 1997 statement, Archbishop Bartholomew, "first among equals" of the Eastern Orthodox Church, called environmental degradation nothing less than sin, something he reiterated in his June 2015 reply to the Catholic Pope Francis's historic encyclical on the environment.[1]

What is sin? Tomes exist examining the topic from every conceivable angle. For our purposes, I'm going with the most basic: Sin is whatever we are responsible for that separates us from God. In other words, it is whatever we do that runs counter to justice and peace, inside and out, according to their richest most inclusive definitions.

Consequently, there's no relationship with God apart from relationships to each other and to the nonhuman natural world under and around us. Considering as we are in this wee book a Jesus beyond Jesus—the repairing incarnation of a loving God deeply interested in a healthy relationship with us—however we damage the earth (with its myriad dependents) is a sin against God. And it is because of that sin that the God of earth dies. Now, I'm not talking about an apocalypse of climatological crisis every year any more than traditional Christians espouse a literal crucifixion of Jesus every year. But it's a way of thinking that should recalibrate our relationship to the earth just as Jesus's death and resurrection recalibrates a Christian's relationship to God.

And then somehow, through that death itself, following this analogy, we may be made right and whole again. The "somehow" and its implications are what occupy traditional Christians for the rest of the year. Because, while it changes everything, some things remain. And while it absolves once and for all, it demands of Christians different ways of thinking and being. These are the paradoxes of traditional Christianity, and they're just as real when we think in terms of a Jesus who includes the earth itself.

Back to compost, then. Its most basic component is death. But in the deep dark of all that deadness, tiny angels are hard at work. Microbes and insects muck about amongst the apple cores and manure, the crispy maple leaves and husks of straw, busily processing the heap into something richly life-giving. If that's not a transformation, I don't know what is.

Then, there we stand on Easter morning before a dark mound, ready for a resurrection.

We, the ordinary and unexceptional, the less-than-impressive, of little account and deeply sad, we come before a perished earth—for what? To pay our respects? To look on it, even dead, and remember better times? To see a shadow of the beloved? Maybe, just maybe, we arrive, whatever our purpose or mix of purposes, with a grain of hope. We approach, hearts beating a little faster for just the hint of the possibility of surprise. The earth, like Jesus, has surprised us so often before and was of all things to be trusted, so why not in its promise to rebuild and still to give life?

The biblical Gospels differ. There are four after all. So when all four agree on something, it's worth taking notice. The Gospels report a consistent feature of Jesus's resurrection appearance, especially notable because any witness had special clout among the survivors. How surprising, then, that every Gospel tells that on the morning after the Sabbath after Jesus's death, a small person of no account—not a disciple, not a governor, not a priest or even a Roman of any repute, but a woman—first witnessed the resurrection. It was Mary from Magdala (either alone or with other women), each Gospel tells, who first learned that Christ was risen.

So, if the analogy holds, should you, whoever you are, approach the place where the crucified God of earth has been taken, with all the conflicted thoughts and emotions of a Mary Magdalene that Easter morning, you may yet see earth alive anew. Perhaps it will be you who glimpses the radiance of an eternal earth shot through with glory.

Will you then run away and astounded say nothing (a la the shorter ending of the Gospel of Mark), or will you fall to the ground, clasping the feet of the God of earth, and worship (a la Matthew)?

And will you, finally, tell others the good news?

Among the most hopeful people I hear talk about climate change and the demise of the nonhuman natural world are paradoxically the very people who are also most vocal about impending catastrophe. Their hope doesn't look like the blind denial that most of us bring to the issue, if we dare look at all, but is of a sort that acknowledges great mystery and power at work in a universe not of our making but under our dominion. Their hope is of a more relational kind, taking joy in what remains and allowing for the possibility that out of it something fresh and wonderful—new life—may yet come.

PART VI

Land Sakes Alive!

"The holiness of the chosen day is not something at which to stare and from which we must humbly stay away. It is holy not *away* from us. It is holy unto us."

—A. J. Heschel

Images of a tender green shoot busting through concrete, butterflies unfurling wings from the mummy of a cocoon, crocuses in snow, fledglings pecking their way from a crusty shell's veneer; any of these would seem to portray the God of earth returned to life. But they ring, if not untrue, then a bit flat, clichéd. None quite attain the depth of analogy with the Christian season of Easter and Pentecost. I'm at a loss to say exactly why.

Maybe it has something to do with the mystical nature of it all: that the traditional Jesus was more than the Jew from Galilee, killed for his troublemaking. His followers maintained that he came back from the dead to walk among them and ascend to heaven, that he was of heaven itself, of God like no other could be; that by some marvel of expiation, he brought faulted human beings back into the good graces of God and in so doing lent us eternal life. That's bigger than bunnies and colored eggs.

Or maybe they don't quite work because previous to each of those admittedly wondrous images, life had not been lost. Earth and the stuff of earth hadn't perished before these instants of renewal transpired but was simply transformed, growing from a fierce life already existing in the seed, the worm, the bulb, the egg. So, lovely as they are, they don't match the amazement of a full vitality following an absolute and utter death.

Maybe it's some combination of those things. After all, if we follow the analogy of traditional Christianity, the God of earth did indeed completely and inarguably die; but this Jesus beyond Jesus also was alive before and continues to live forever after. The God of earth, a dynamic and complex creation of interrelated life, was before and is alive again. What makes the God of earth not exactly the same as earth is belief that this Jesus-beyond-Jesus, Jesus enduring as the God of earth, is the intentional incarnation of a God who desires that things be right, repaired between us.

The annual return of each season corresponding to the moments of Jesus's life reflects this reality—simultaneously the reality of each moment and its opportunity to remember and reflect. The moments are not absolute according to a linear system in time but recur and, in their recurrence, invite us to participate in a mystery.

Exploring the resurrected God of earth in light of the traditional season of Easter and Pentecost is, in some ways, the most difficult to manage of all analogies to the Christian calendar. It's the least logical, yet the most crucial. It's like glimpsing another dimension that despite the blinding of our habits or our grief has been and is there right along. But like those grail-seeking knights or fairy-tale heroes, we can see only after we've surrendered and allowed the God of earth to shift something in ourselves. In other words, it's not a fact but a relationship.

This is the point in this project's experiment that most surprised me with a flash of deepest comfort and joy. I wish I could say that the insight sticks, that my heart has held fast in clarity to that great grace. Maybe for you it will, it does. For me, it's a fleeting thing—glimpses and flickers—but even its recollection takes the edge off despair.

16

The Comedy of Surprise

"i thank You God for most this amazing
day: for the leaping greenly spirits of trees"

—e. e. cummings

"Motley young savages . . . more-or-less a biker gang," that's
how a local journalist described the community he visited near
Lynchburg, Virginia.[1] For most people around here, "Lynchburg" evokes notions more consonant with conservative, evan-
gelical Christians a la Jerry Falwell's Liberty University or the
genteel equestriennes of Sweet Briar College. A lot of Civil War
history can be found there (Lynchburg was never captured by
the Union army). Otherwise it's a pretty quiet, pretty place in
a pastoral idyll of old America.

Lynchburg is not where I'd imagine a counterculture of tat-
tooed ex-cons living in an intentional community espousing
not only a radical independence from a capitalist economy but
also a radical ethic of spirituality and environmental sustainability. Not really. Nope, not at all. Yet there they are, the
Wolves of Vinland. They've been there for nearly ten years
and show no signs of leaving. On the contrary, the community
begun by brothers Mattias and Paul Waggoner has grown to
include over 300 members and has chapters out West, too.

Paul reports that for years beforehand, they lived on the
ragged edge of illegal drugs, parasitic relationships, and general

"bad-assery" until "we realized we were expending our creative energies in the wrong direction. We wanted to find a better, more sustainable way of life, one that wouldn't compromise our personal integrity." They sought "an honorable mode of living." So, they looked around and settled in. They harvested logs, prepared the wood, and constructed several off-grid houses. Members grow much of their own food and trade or barter for other necessities. "We wanted to create a community oriented about shared values of sustainability and self-reliance . . . a dynamic of power share versus power drain."[2]

Whatever else one might think about the Wolves, there's a resurrection in their story. For the people's part, it's intentional, an attitude, a choice in ways of being and ways of seeing. It's the difference between using a material earth, consuming for individual self-interest, and recognizing a relationship with the earth built on gratitude and respect. In the vocabulary of this book, it's a recognition of the God of earth, risen from the dead, with healing in her wings. It's attention to the possibility of a Jesus beyond Jesus immediate and alive, extending the offer of life-giving relationship(s) through the nonhuman natural world.

And so it is that in the most unlikely and desperate of circumstances, grace appears. Possibility squeezes in where it seemed there couldn't possibly be room. Hope is appropriate, mystery is for real. Our knowledge and expectations may not be adequate to the capacity the God of earth has to surprise us with beauty, healing, inspiration, and joy. This is not a Pollyannaish optimism or meant to promote a laissez-faire attitude toward ecological devastation, but rather draws upon the spiritual discipline of hope, even in the face of global warming, fracking, and subsidized factory farming—that another, better way may suddenly become real, that despite everything, the earth as the incarnation of God is alive again.

And there's more. By analogy with the resurrection of Jesus, this life-again is life for us. The God of earth is immediate, material, and flesh-fresh. Out of death, a living land with life to offer. That's the gospel of the God of earth.

I call this chapter a "comedy" in the manner of old theater, when a play was defined as either a tragedy, wherein things didn't work out, or a comedy, where they did. In other words, the category is not defined by laugh aloud humor or snicker-snicker jokes but by the quality of the end—sad or happy. Resurrection of our hero surely qualifies as happy. But there's more at work in the story of a Jesus beyond Jesus in the God of earth. There's the element of surprise, a surprise so outlandish that we just might miss it.

If we track the God of earth's story according to its biblical and traditional analogy, what transpires isn't predictable or remotely logical. Something the Gospel stories have in common is disbelief, specifically the disbelief of Jesus's most intimate companions, the men who hung on his words and to whom he had even said that he would return. In some Gospels, the disciples' initial disbelief is compounded by a striking failure even to see or to recognize the risen Jesus when he stood again among them.

I confess that the more I learn about how human activity is altering the planet, how our willful ignorance and greed are pushing out millions of individuals and thousands of species in what scientists are calling a "great extinction"—*The Sixth Extinction*, as detailed in Elizabeth Kolbert's Pulitzer Prize–winning book—on the order of earlier, geological events (and the first caused by human beings), the less optimistic I am that we can turn this thing around. So let me be perfectly clear: what follows in no way gets us off the hook. But here it is: the God of earth, crucified and dead-dead, can come, *has* come back to life.

The death is still there. But so is new life. A caveat (and this is hugely important): this is not an objective fact so much as a subjective truth.

At issue is attitude; our attitude. It is to recognize with the intention of decision, even in the face of planetary destruction, the God of earth alive among us. It's a different quality of life than the daily secular, as real as any but richer, too. Call it eternal, divine: it's the life of the risen Christ with God the Creator through whom we are saved.

In order to unpack what all that means and its implications in the context of the God of earth, I have to add this: We must believe. That's a crucial ingredient for the implications of resurrection. "How is it we can't accept this," the poet Charles Wright writes, "that all trees were holy once, / that all light is altar light."[3] It's so hard to do. And what does it mean to believe, anyway? The God of earth arisen is, and not simply newly alive, but like the traditional Jesus, offers new life to us, too.

"Nature conceals her mystery by means of her essential grandeur, not by her cunning," said Albert Einstein. Two men walked a good while with the risen Jesus without recognizing him; Mary thought he was the gardener at first; and the disciples needed proof, most famously Thomas, whom Jesus invited to poke the nail holes in Jesus's hands and to put his hand into the wound in Jesus's side. The risen Jesus talked, walked, fished, and ate with them—all mundane and concretely embodied activities. Sure, Jesus praised those "who have not seen and yet have come to believe,"[3] but even for those who had loved Jesus and known him best of all, it took relationship with the re-embodied Christ for them to accept the good news.

Even in the face of the despair of those who know the earth best—biologists tracking the Arctic's changing ecosystems; humanitarian aid workers in Bangladesh grappling with the ravages of a rising sea; ornithologists searching for macaws in a shrinking rainforest; the organic farmer battling the spread of GMO seeds from neighboring farms; the mountain climber at her peak, gazing down brokenhearted at a coal-ravaged range—we are called to believe.

How can we, who witness the crucifixion of the God of earth, believe in her life renewed?

I have long struggled to reconcile my knowledge of the effects of human assault on the planet with a desire to live with joy. Maybe this is how: the Easter of the God of earth. It's a new way of looking at the earth and my relationship to it. And not simply looking, but actively engaging with wholehearted joy the reality of the God of earth alive. It doesn't erase or otherwise ignore the devastation, my part in it, and my responsibility to try to correct or at least not exacerbate; but it charges me also to acknowledge, to recognize, the mystery of a God of earth right here in relationship to me, who despite our gravest assassination, is alive. But I cannot experience that except by recognizing, by coming to believe that it is so. Faith in what is unseen within the whirling green splendor of earth—life eternal.

But we must be open. We must choose (hesitantly or wholeheartedly, it doesn't matter) to believe, to allow for the reality of the God of earth. Then, by the grace of an immediate earth—the wonder of the world in its most concrete, most embodied, most physical around, over, and under us—we might discover God's dynamic, loving self. In such relationship, by our honoring the possibility of earth as the incarnation of a God who desires life for us and for all; by such faith we might be saved. In the depth of our recognition, stumbling upon, aha even a glimpse of the God of earth's enduring vitality, beauty, and love, we might be reconciled to all that is holy, and live.

"I believe that out of an erotics of place, a politics of place is emerging," Terry Tempest Williams writes. "Not radical, but conservative, a politics rooted in empathy . . . the enterprise of conservation is a revolution, an evolution of the spirit."[4]

The crucifixion of the God of earth is a rejection of its holiness, its intrinsic value. It's a violent disrespect for the earth's mind-blowing power and beauty, the blatant disregard for a sacred quality permeating the nonhuman natural world. Easter doesn't erase the crucifixion, but it transforms its meaning. This triumphant moment is occasion to recognize that the holiness of earth endures and with that, transforms us. In our recognizing that the God of earth is alive, in our daring to believe in that vitality, is joy and life renewed. It's a mystery how this can be—that despite the worst havoc we wreak against the God of earth, nevertheless, he is alive. And not just alive but extending, through belief in her vitality, redemption: full life reconciled to all that is holy, "to everything which is natural which is infinite which is yes," e. e. cummings wrote.[5]

The thing about such recognition is that it cannot be an end in itself. It must be shared, and I don't mean simply because it is compelling but because its realization is not purely a personal, individualistic matter. Rather, it is complete only when shared, which develops, corrects, and reinvigorates the recognition. The risen God of earth actively inspires this dynamic give-and-take.

17
Now, Go; and Be Here

"As kingfishers catch fire, dragonflies draw flame."
—Gerard Manley Hopkins

Say something.

I am not activist material. A small woman from laconic people, I spend most of my time alone muttering just loudly enough to get the dogs barking in suspicion that another person (egads) may be approaching. What's more, I am averse to conflict—strongly. Such qualities an effective activist do not make. Yet there's no getting around it. After the privilege of witnessing the God of earth's vitality and endurance sinks in, comes the charge. Tongues of fire.

"We've killed the earth, / Yet we speak of other things," poet Chase Twichell writes. "What etiquette holds us back / from more intimate speech, especially now, at the end of the world?"[1] It's hard for most of us to speak up, to speak out against the norm, against what's popular or convenient or accepted. Impossible even . . . unless one's heart is in it. (And ah, there's the grace, the spirit of the thing.)

I was in the thick of grad school myopia, attending to little other than researching aberrations in ancient Hebrew, theories of tribal confederacy, and figuring out how to make my computer write from right to left, bending every effort of will to getting my dissertation underway. Yet one event remarkably able to cut through that morass was an act undertaken clear across the country by another small woman, young, and very alone. Alone, that is, in terms of human collaboration. She did have a partner in her crime—Luna, of quiet demeanor and great strength, 180 feet tall and 1,400 years old, a tree as old as the Masoretic text I studied.

In the strength, and plight, of Luna, Julia Butterfly Hill spoke out. And the message got around. One day in 1997, Ms. Hill volunteered to sit in an ancient redwood tree in order to slow Pacific Lumber Company's clear-cutting through these irreplaceable forests. And she stayed high in the branches of that tree despite storms both human and meteorological for over two years—until not only was Luna saved but also all the trees within a 200-foot buffer zone, and efforts were undertaken toward more sustainable forestry in the region.

"Courage," Julia Butterfly Hill notes on her webpage, comes from the word for "heart," the French *coeur*.[2] Even in the face of overwhelming scientific evidence that we human beings are damaging our planet, people call for more—more tests, more studies, more expert witness to convince us why we must change our fossil-fuel-dependent *M.O.* Courage. It's no longer a matter of head, it's a matter of heart. In order to shift, in order to "repent," to borrow the biblical language, we must change our hearts. Those with heart must, from the heart, speak.

"I am a scientist," Barbara Kingsolver writes, "who thinks it wise to enter the doors of creation . . . with the reverence humankind has traditionally summoned for entering places of worship."[3] Yes, we need all the careful qualitative studies, sophisticated biological monitoring, and chemical analysis that impeccably trained scientists can bring. But evidence suggests that evidence is not enough. So, Mardy Murie, a small woman whose livelihood depended on the scientific work of biology, appealed at a hearing concerning the Alaskan Lands Bill, not out of her considerable expertise. "I am testifying," she said, "as

an emotional woman. . . . Beauty is a resource in and of itself."[4]
Beauty is a thing of the heart.

The disciples of Jesus believed in their heart of hearts that
they had good news. This moment in the cycle of the God of
earth corresponds to Pentecost, a Christian phenomenon with
ancient Jewish roots.

Torah. The word is frequently translated "law." But most
people who read biblical Hebrew agree that "instruction" is
a more consistently accurate translation, based both on ety-
mology and context of use. Linguistics aside, Torah is not a
burden, but a gift. So the moment when God graced human
beings with the Torah is a moment to remember with joy . . .
and cheese blintzes. The Jewish festival of Shavuot celebrates
God's giving human beings instructions for how best to be in
relation to each other, to the world around, and to God. Torah
is the Word of God—in Greek, the *logos*. Of Torah, Moses
said that it is no less than life itself. But it didn't come auto-
matically. Rather, people had, have, a choice—to accept it or
not. "Choose life!" Moses urged.

The Christian moment of Pentecost, depending on and
reflecting its Jewish roots with Moses at Mount Sinai, recalls an
equally dramatic investment of God's Word into human experience. Jesus had promised his disciples that his ascension wouldn't
be an abandonment. On the contrary, he would send his Spirit
to be with and in them. So it was that on one Jewish Shavuot a
rushing wind filled the place where the disciples had gathered.
Then fire—individual tongues of it—rested on each one.

Thus "filled with the Holy Spirit," the disciples spoke out,
enabled to do so in all variety of foreign languages. The message was for the world, the biblical story tells, and the Spirit
enabled them to communicate regardless of their audience's
nationality. "Repent and be baptized," that's what the disciples said, and they promised happy consequences: forgiveness
and inspiration. To repent is turn—turn from something bad

toward something better. To be baptized was to recognize this new way of living, new way of being. It was, with its attendant reconciliation to God, to "be saved."

I have real issues with the traditional Christian zeal behind missionary efforts that smack of arrogance and colonialism; but the point remains at its most naked: with hearts on fire from the good news of God's exacting salvation through God's own incarnation on earth, the disciples were charged to speak, to announce and explain that anyone could be reconciled to heaven and share in the fullest life.

By analogy, those who experience something of the sacredness of earth, who recognize in it an enduring and intrinsic value (whatever language they may use), even the complexity and beauty of the fullness of life itself, are charged to say something, no matter how small and solitary we may feel.

It's a charge that burns with good news.

Repent and be baptized. Assault against the earth that compromises its wellness compromises the wellness of all who dwell within it, now and into the future. If anything is a sin, this surely qualifies. Recognizing the God of earth, alive among us and bearing the capacity to reconcile and heal compels us to call out for change—to turn from an ecologically destructive lifestyle toward sustainability—and to live out that change with a new perspective, new ways of being.

Repent.

I'm not talking about petrified notions of repentance from some obscure religious guilt or about a traditional baptism in font or river. But the turning of heart and actions from the hurtful to the good, and through that turning of entrance into a different way of living, of being, that's what I'm talking about.

And be saved.

The happy news is that in such repentance is absolution and life. "It is a wholesome and necessary thing for us to turn again to the earth," said biologist Rachel Carson, "and in the contemplation of her beauties to know of wonder and humility."[5] That's the promise, the joy, and it compels those who recognize it to speak out.

Dear Congresswoman, please support improvements to rail service in order that people can move about with less cost to the planet. . . . Dear President, please honor limitations of use in our National Parks. . . . Dear Senator, please divert subsidies from mega agribusiness to small family farms. . . . Dear Governor, please create jobs renovating for energy efficiency. . . . Dear Monsanto, please retire your drug-addicted seeds. . . . Dear grocery store owner, please provide incentives for customers to bring reusable containers and bags. . . . Dear office of public utilities, please discourage new oil wells, power lines, and pipelines. . . . Dear leaders of the G8, come on! . . . Dear neighbor, thank you for your crazy native plant yard, which is beautiful as are your blue jeans and boxer shorts blowing on the clothesline.

"I am asking you as members of this subcommittee, as my lawmakers, my guardians of justice, for one favor," Terry Tempest Williams said in her 1991 testimony concerning the management of the Pacific yew, with its possible cancer-fighting potency. "Will you please go visit the trees? . . . Think. . . . Think. . . . Think about how our sacred texts may be found in the forest as well as in the Psalms, and then, my dear lawmakers, I ask you to make your decision with your heart."[6]

Say something.

I'm inclined to end here, with this charge to speak out. But there's something else. For ours is not the only or even final word. Listen. Inasmuch as the risen God of earth has inspired us to cry, "Repent!" we are also audience to such a call.

Disciples of the God of earth aren't limited to human beings. The nonhuman natural world, filled with the Spirit of the God of earth, also cries, "Repent!" From the Colorado River's valiant terminus, struggling to saturate its formerly lush delta's cracked surface, to great masses of coral quietly bleaching as they perish beneath warming oceans, from the hummingbird exhausted in its search for nesting ground to the larvae of a blue swallowtail butterfly aborted by regional mosquito spraying, aspects and inhabitants of this blue-green planet home are also calling, calling, calling. "Repent!" they say, "and be saved."

PART VII

Living the Ordinary after All

"Before enlightenment, chop wood, carry water. After enlightenment, chop wood, carry water."

—popular Zen saying

Having glimpsed a redemptive divinity in earth, having recognized a Jesus beyond Jesus in the nonhuman natural world and witnessed the God of earth's endurance despite even death, the days still come and go with more than enough trouble and pain. So, how do we deal? How do we live? Same, but different.

The traditional church's seasons of "Ordinary Time" lie outside the most dramatic moments in Jesus's biblical story. They are the times for daily life, for all that is mundane and humdrum. In the first period, before Jesus's death, they were days of building relationships, of challenge and learning, of savoring the company of God made flesh. Scriptures for that period recall the adult Jesus's day-to-day dealings on earth. This second period, after Jesus's death and ascension and before his coming again, is likewise of the day-to-day. They are days of struggling to hang on to a glimpsed truth, of work commensurate with new knowledge, of anxiety and hope.

In other words, these periods are the very most relevant and pressing and immediate for us even in all their, well, ordinariness.

Ordinary time is about the God of earth not in some wow-look-at-that sort of moment or realization but in all of every bit of what it means to be a universal, timeless God so deeply committed to reconciling us and so enamored of the stuff of granite and jack pines and praying mantises and manatees and osprey and clear blue ice and small mouth bass and reindeer and tree frogs as to become of it all. Ordinary time is time for us to really dive in and grapple with what it all means for the business of life on earth. Like the human Jesus's disciples, we are left to ask "How now shall we live?" We come face-to-face, head on with the implications and responsibilities of being the image of God on earth to have dominion and be, male and female, *adam,* in relation to *adamah,* "brother's keeper" and worshipful attendants of the dynamic and multifaceted world that we have come quite remarkably to inhabit.

This is the long haul. Faith falters and doubt gets the upper hand. The world shrinks to mere stuff, holiness fades, and the colors go flat. The world seems filled with hypocrites, myself chief among them, and still I feel alone, scrambling for a foothold in a landslide of greed and myopia. At such times, we do well to remember, there's this: others, lots of others, millions of others who recognize holiness in the earth and have experienced redemption through a wild grace. The community of the faithful will buoy us up, instruct and encourage, chastise when correction is in order and perhaps most important of all, locate joy.

After all, all of this is consecrated time, the year in God-of-earth-i-ness, with its own challenges and responsibilities yes, but despite it all and at the foundation of it all—joy.

18

Wonder and Works, or a Gardener's Peculiar Constitution

"The ultimate goal of farming is not the growing of crops, but the cultivation and perfection of human beings."
—Masanobu Fukuoka

They're black as black can be and of a speck size so tiny that you really can't pinch only one at a time from your palm. Basil seeds. Every year, I buy a packet. Crouching at the base of scraggly tomato transplants, I run my finger through far-too-clumpy soil to push out a shallow trough. Then, usually with damp and dirty gloves, I try to sprinkle with some consistency of application, just a few seeds at a time along the row.

Try as I might, I know I'm pinching gobs of seeds sometimes and probably none at other times. I don't know for sure because as soon as they fall, they disappear, despite the aid of my bottle-bottom, progressive lens spectacles. I really can't be sure the seeds landed where I intended. Oh, well. With the edge of my palm, I push on the trough (seeds or no seeds) lightly, pull a thin blanket of soil over the top, tamp down the line, and sprinkle the area with my old watering can, itself less than optimal. (The dog, in his youth, chewed the sprinkler end, so now the water barely comes out on the right side and in a pummeling stream on the left. "Sprinkling," in other words, is a bit of a misnomer.)

For some reason, every year, I do this all in haste as if my not attending closely expunges the utter imperfection of the task. And every year, when I'm done, I turn my back on the plot certain that the seeds won't come up. There is no way. Not only are they impossibly small and each so very hard, but also my planting technique, if one could call it that, does not at all conform to the package instructions. Indeed, for far longer than you'd think it should take if the seeds were really going to germinate, the ground around the tomatoes remains bare.

Just as I thought, I think. This is the year the basil doesn't grow.

And then it does.

Tiny dark green leaves hunker close to the soil surface and of a peculiar shape, all basil's own. I recognize them, now, and within the next couple of days my pattern of planting emerges. Clumps here, a loner there and there. But always there are far, far more tiny seedlings than I need, and each one is one more than I expected.

If we are indeed "saved by faith," what's the point of "works"? Judging from the biblical record, this question in several dimensions preoccupied the earliest Christians. Paul worried the question like a youngster does a scab, and no one has solved it, once and for all, since. I was raised Lutheran. So when I dutifully plopped my awkward adolescent self down with my fellow confirmation students on Wednesday nights, I got Luther's take on the issue—the Diet of Worms (snicker snicker), 95 Theses, "baptized anew every day"—"by faith *alone*," he audaciously added to Paul.[1] It confirmed the problem, as much as anything.

People sometimes point out the apparent biblical discrepancy between Paul's prioritizing faith and James's prioritizing works, appealing for Paul's part to Galatians 2:16 and Romans 3:28 versus James 2:24 and 26. Paul writes of justification not by "works of the law" but by faith in/of Jesus; while James writes that like the body needs the spirit, so faith needs works to be a truly living faith. Even accepting that they're talking about different kinds of "works"—flat, line-by-line obligations (Paul), versus simply doing the right thing, charitable or otherwise (James)—that they're having the discussion at all reveals an intriguing dynamism between these two crucial elements, faith and works.

In the context of the God of earth, consider this: Doing the right thing environmentally (and by so doing, actively caring for others present and future) is super important. Works. What is the right thing environmentally may seem a complicated matter to determine. A good place to start is simply trying to live with less—less stuff, yes; but primarily less consumption of fossil fuel. It's finding the sweet spot of need, and making that one's want, for starters. But doing so can feel like a chore, deprivation, and flatly unfair in the face of other choices: spacious vehicles, distant vacations, big homes at a perfectly consistent comfortable temperature, any kind of food any time of year no matter where one lives. To make the right choice environmentally, simply because we *should*, can end up in resentment at best. Enter, faith.

It becomes infinitely easier with a different relationship to the earth—when we have faith, that is, when we experience the saving grace of the God of earth, a Jesus beyond Jesus infusing the nonhuman natural world around. Call it re-enchantment, imagination, enlightenment, or simply humble awareness; and appreciate that that quality is the product of a loving God's desire to give us peace. That's faith in/of the God of earth. The "works," then, simply follow. In this context, they may actually be more like non-works, characterized as they are more by desisting and stillness than by large-scale activity. The countercultural, rather shocking paradox is that such an approach can be cause for deep satisfaction, peace, and even joy.

But what would the GDP look like, an audience member asked, if we were we to reduce our use of fossil fuels enough to bring the CO_2 in the atmosphere back down to 350 parts per million?[2] Bill McKibben's answer first allowed how difficult such a thing is to predict. A lot can happen between now and then to affect such a number. We do know, McKibben said, "that it's affordable, at least compared to not doing it." But finally, he pressed, there's another, deeper matter at stake in the question.

What if an ever higher GDP doesn't actually make us happy? McKibben observed, "While [the GDP] has trebled in the last 50 years, the percentage of Americans who pronounce themselves 'very satisfied' with their lives has gone steadily down . . . only a quarter of Americans." We've been so preoccupied with having "bigger houses farther apart" that "the average American has half as many close friends as the average American 50 years ago." He concluded by saying, "I'd rather [my daughter] try to measure [friendships]," McKibben said, "than figure out exactly how much stuff she's going to be carrying around."[3]

Masanobu Fukuoka lived most of his long adult life (he died at 95) as a farmer, specifically tending a small plot of land in Japan, the few acres spared to him after World War II when American forces redistributed such real estate. He rebelled against modern farming practices, choosing instead to work as much in alliance with whatever the natural inclinations of his space—the soil and its inhabitants—were. In the process, he developed a philosophy of farming without tilling, pruning, or the use of chemicals that came to be called simply "natural farming" or (my favorite) "do-nothing farming." "I am fortunate to have grown rice and barley," Fukuoka said. "Only to him who stands where the barley stands, and listens well, will it speak and tell, for his sake, what man is."[4]

Works, in this God of earth model, begin then to look more like the reverent care and keeping that human beings, according to the Bible, were originally set in God's garden to do—a purpose that afforded deep satisfaction and comfort, a definition to being, and fullness of life.

19

Judgment and Mercy

"Sometimes
I go about pitying myself
While I am carried by
The wind
Across the sky."

—Chippewa song

I'd like to say that I broke up with my long-distance boyfriend because I couldn't bear the cost to the planet of my desire to be with him. I'd like to say that in a moment of ecological integrity, I chose the sacrifice of a monk, put aside my singular wants for the greater good. I didn't. I simply fell in love with someone else closer to home. Sure, add to that the mundane reasons: too far for too long, the proverbial toothpaste cap, and so on. But I cannot say that I quit the regular plane flights and long car trips for environmental reasons. As a matter of fact, I married and promptly moved to a city seventy-five miles from my work. Seventy-five miles. Plus, the house where we live requires that I drive absolutely anywhere I might need to go beyond our home. What's more, it has acres of lawn over which a team of men ride fuel-chugging mowers several times a month through the summer. Mea culpa. Forgive me Father, it has been a lifetime since my last confession.

And yet. Still, the sun shines on my back, the Asian pear puts out its fruit, and I am comforted by the sound of a clear stream rushing past my feet, its flow eddying around my ankles.

I return to the earth, chastised and penitent; and sometimes I find there simply mercy.

I did resign my tenured post in part because I couldn't justify environmentally the long drive but also because my husband encourages and supports my decisions and work. I can now walk to my office—a few feet across the driveway—and the Boss Lady in my head gives me occasional leave to garden, when the season is right and I can tend the space around as responsibly as I can muster. We've improved the insulation and tightened some windows, transitioned a chunk of lawn to flowers, trees, and other things delicious and beautiful. But I am far from righteous.

I eat meat, drive without much hesitation, turn the thermostat up during cold times, and on and on. I am not without sin. "To use or not to use nature is not a choice that is available to us," Wendell Berry writes. "We can live only at the expense of other lives."[1] But that is no excuse, no absolution, no justification. Merely fact.

Justification by faith, those are the terms of this experiment, anyway. But what does that mean? What does that mean in terms of a Jesus beyond Jesus, in terms of the God of earth? The biblical Jesus preached a demanding message—lots of love, sure, but then there were also the sheep and the goats, the good soil and the bad, the adulterous glance, that give-up-all-you-have business. "I have come not to abolish [the law]," Jesus said, "but to fulfill [it]."[2]

And after Jesus had gone away to heaven, in the period of this second Ordinary Time, expectation and judgment remain and intensify. On the day of judgment, Paul says, "[God] will repay according to what each has done": to the good, life; to the self-seeking who reject truth, wrath and distress.[3] Revelation's white-horse horseman—called Faithful and True, the Word of God, and King of Kings—wears a bloody robe and spouts a sword the better to "tread the wine press of the fury of the wrath of God."[4] Such judgment is bound to be a punishing matter, to say the least.

We cannot live in this world without bearing some degree of culpability, and when judgment determines guilt, justice demands punishment—a correction born by the guilty to repay the cost of the crime. That's the ideal of justice without which, the sages tell, there is no peace.

There is but one alternative to punishment: mercy. Forgiveness is an active choice of the wronged party to move into a reconciled future without exacting the punishment due. On the field of justice, this is mercy. And in the little religious corner where this book plays, faith is a mercy. We are justified, the Christian theologians tell, by faith.

By analogy to the traditional Jesus, it is faith in the God of earth. Extending Jesus beyond Jesus to include earth itself, the God of earth forgives us, absolves us, and washes us clean—if we would just believe. We are justified by faith—belief that the Creator God who stands outside of time and beyond the beyond has chosen to be present to us and with us through the material stuff of earth in order that we might be reconciled to her.

And that brings us back to the subject of the previous chapter. Such faith is not an end in itself but is yoked to works—to our own subjectivity and freedoms. It compels us toward certain ways of being and doing. Recognizing and accepting the forgiveness that the God of earth extends by mercy and grace orients us to be in the world for a greater good.

I wish I could unhear the damningly true analogy a gentle friend of mine made in conversation some time ago. She talked about how she wrestled with her own fossil fuel use, knowing what we know of its destructive consequences. We sat in a café in an old neighborhood, about half a mile from where white people bought and sold black people. "Our dependence on fossil fuels is like slavery in the South," she said. "All those decent, God-fearing people, who saw that their economy would collapse if they dared to acknowledge the personhood of blacks."

"Do you love me?" Jesus asked his most devoted disciple, Peter. The biblical story in John 21 tells that Peter was crestfallen that Jesus should ask such a question at all. But Jesus was getting after more than warm cuddly feelings. "Then feed my sheep," Jesus said. And so the God of earth charges us, calls us to act for others out of love for the specific.

It sounds easy but demands everything we've got. Just as "my sheep" means more than the literal fuzzy four-legged ruminants of the world to extend to all God's creatures now and into the future, so "feed" means more than stuffing the belly. It is a sophisticated, learned matter that demands the best science twinned with wisest ethics and enlivened with heart in order that all beings now and in the future have what they need—food, sure, but also clean air, the space and peace to live fully, and beauty too—not merely for one species of one color today, but for all and for all time to come.

The God of earth's charge to "feed my sheep" is not a one-size-fits-all proposition, then. Observing the necessity of our using the beings and resources around us, Wendell Berry writes, "Our choice has rather to do with how and how much to use . . . it must be worked out in local practice because, by necessity, the practice will vary somewhat from one locality to another. There is, thus, no *practical* way that we can intend the good of the world; practice can only be local."[5] We have a choice. We make choices every day.

The ones who suffer most and for whom it will only get worse, climate scientists say, are the ones who have done least if anything to contribute to the problem. They are the disenfranchised and voiceless of the world from the black rhino to the Bangladeshi rickshaw driver, from the manatee to the subsistence fisherman with his small dory and handheld net, from the Maasai mother to the Shenandoah salamander. These are the biblical "widow and orphan," of course. These are Jesus's sheep.

And every day I fail them. Every day, in the leisure of my wealth, I contribute to the sin that demands a reckoning. And if judgment is measured by increasingly intense storms, crises of drought and wildfire, flooding and heat, then it is here and as much a collective guilt that we bear as it is individual.

If that's all there was to say about it, we might just as well give up and give in. But that isn't all. That's not where such thinking can end.

After all, taking into account the sources of harm emboldens us to see that inasmuch as we each bear our own guilt, vastly more problematic are the costs of corporate greed and national agendas. To slip into despair because I eat meat sometimes, drive a car, and occasionally use plastic bags; to say that the planet is in peril primarily because of my neighbor's SUV or my sister's air conditioning is a gross failure of perspective. Worse, it runs the risk of letting the monumental offenders continue conducting business as usual while we nitpick critiques of each other.

Despite failure, we are compelled by faith to live in the truth of our justification and try, try to make choices about how we use what we use, choices that are wise and generous, that limit the scope of our destruction, the cost of our wants. Because once we're done with a litany of sins—mine, and yours too while we're at it, where does that leave us? *Now* what are we going to do? Every day, the offer is extended of forgiveness and faith. And out of that faith, to do better. And when we fail, still the God of earth absolves . . . if we would but believe.

20

With Wild Delight, a Mandate for Joy

"In the presence of nature, a wild delight runs though the man, in spite of real sorrows. Nature says,—he is my creature, and maugre all his impertinent griefs, he shall be glad with me."

—Ralph Waldo Emerson

"In spite of": that's what *maugre* means. In spite of, notwithstanding all the sorrow, all the grief, stands the God of earth, arms full of wonder, with gladness and peace. Come what may, good news remains.

As a boy subject to the sexual predation of a well-respected acquaintance, Barry Lopez took comfort in even the most demeaning moments of abuse by the "sliver of sky" that he could see from the man's bed. Through the long period of trauma and in the decades that followed, Lopez found succor and salvation in the wild. "The deepest and sometimes only relief I had," Lopez writes, "was when I was confronted with the local, elementary forces of nature. . . . I took from each of these encounters a sense of what it might feel like to become fully alive . . . Encouragement."[1]

The stuff of earth didn't miraculously intercede, say in a cosmic earthquake that brought the roof down on Harry Shier, Lopez's abuser, to free the boy forever. An eagle didn't fly in through the window to pluck out the man's eyes while a wolf from the stairs unmanned Shier in some super Hollywood vindication. No. But the "sliver of sky" was there, and

Lopez found a way in connection to it to endure. He has since become one of our most brilliant observers and poignant essayists of the natural world.

I suspect that you have your own experience, I hope less traumatic but no less powerful, of comfort, delight, surprise, encouragement, or inspiration from the nonhuman natural world. May such experiences be many for you and for your children and your children's children, too.

A recent study strongly suggests that, given our own incarnate natures, awe and beauty actually affect our immune systems, boosting immunity and anti-inflammatory responses. "That awe, wonder, and beauty promote healthier levels of cytokines suggests that the things we do to experience these emotions— taking a walk in nature, losing oneself in music, beholding art—have a direct influence upon health and life expectancy."[2]

In the context of the God of earth, in this final period of Ordinary Time analogous to the Christian calendar, we live in the reality of God's choosing to become of earth—in and through the nonhuman natural world. We accept the truth of God's enduring vitality, even when the incarnation that redeems feels far away indeed. "Earth's crammed with heaven," the poet Elizabeth Barrett Browning writes, "And every common bush afire with God. / But only he who sees takes off his shoes . . ."[3] How do we recognize the incarnation of God— alive, still—within the stuff of earth itself?

Just as the first Christians after Jesus's ascension strove to work out what the Jesus-of-Nazareth event meant for them theologically and practically, in relation to each other and to the world around, so we are called to be intentional about how to live in light of the life, death, and resurrection of the God of earth. I can't say exactly what that looks like in absolutist or universal terms. It's hard enough for me to glimpse, merely ever so often, the possibility of that truth. Of only this I'm sure: it's a relationship thing.

"Love one another," Jesus commanded his followers before he died, "even as I have loved you." How does the God of earth love? How can we love like that? George Washington Carver said, "If a person walks in the woods and listens carefully, he can learn more than what is in books, for they speak with the voice of God."[4] Studying the ways of the nonhuman natural world can teach us a lot, even, I submit, how best to love one another. This is the ongoing work of Ordinary Time, the task that's never done but a vocation unto itself.

Meanwhile, in the hard and often discouraging business of seeking a more sustainable environmental ethic, of loving as the God of earth loves, it's easy to lose sight of the whole point. Even in realizing a way of being that promotes the flourishing health of the wildly interconnected natural world, of which we are a part, it's easy to lose sight of joy. Yet it's blessedly crucial to a relationship to the God of earth. To all us Protestant work-ethic folks, I say it's a responsibility, joy. And while no one can give it, it's there for the taking. Take it we should.

"There is nothing I can give you which you have not got," begins a sixteenth century letter from one Fra Giovanni Giocondo to "the Most Illustrious the Contessina Allagia Dela Aldobrandeschi."

> But there is much, very much, that, while I cannot give it, you can take. No Heaven can come to us unless our hearts find rest in it to-day. Take Heaven! No peace lies in the future which is not hidden in this present little instant. Take peace! The gloom of the world is but a shadow. Behind it, yet within our reach, is joy. There is radiance and glory in the darkness, could we but see; and to see, we have only to look. Contessina, I beseech you to look.[5]

Just as we have a responsibility to do what we can to embrace and adopt the wisdoms of earth, to do the right thing, given our place on and relationship to the planet, so I believe we have a responsibility for joy. We are called by the God of earth to revel in her delights, to stand in wonder and awe, to take pleasure where pleasure is to be had, and to live as if we know and know for certain that a fierce and wise love is at work in and through the world around us, a love that reconciles us to heaven even as it nestles us in earth.

In the ordinary moments of our ordinary days, we are called to enjoy what health our bodies bear, to seize what beauty is there for the taking (and no less for our seizing), to savor food secured and prepared with wisdom, to delight in the companionship of others human and nonhuman, to be unreserved in allowing the riches around and within us to give us joy. We have a responsibility for that, too, just as much as a responsibility to correct the damage and redirect destructive practices. I am not an activist. I lack the courage and feel depleted and defeated by standing up and standing out on unpopular, non-mainstream issues. So it is with special glee and no little comfort that I recognize this other side, this joy-despite aspect of honoring the God of earth.

What is it that you love, that gives you pleasure, and softens your heart with joy? Your kids? Then be with them. Not with gizmos, the distractions of driving, or in the frantic context of an amusement park or mall. But simply *with* them to talk, or not, but to allow the space simply to be and to see one another. Do you love food? Then learn about it, delight in what is healthy for you and the planet. Music? Let it flood and fill you. Create, if that's your thing, or simply support the artists who are spending their precious lives in pursuit not of the production of more cheap junk and the biggest fastest dollar but in the ultimately ephemeral and transitory nature of sound, the play of color and shape. There is such extraordinary joy to be had that not only doesn't depend on devastating consumption but actually affords respite from it.

And the angels sing, "Glory!" The angels sing "peace."

The end of the second Ordinary Time leans toward expectation, the expectation of Jesus's coming again. Corresponding New Testament writings reflect apocalyptic expectation as Jesus's followers awaited the world's end. Then, according to the Hebrew prophet Isaiah, there would be "new heavens, a new earth."[6]

But the cosmic collapse didn't come, not as the first- and second-century Christians had defined it. Instead, "with the woes of sin and strife / the world has suffered long / beneath the angel-strain have rolled / two thousand years of wrong." Edmund Sears wrote into his carol "It Came Upon the Midnight Clear" an evocative image of Isaiah's new world. "The age of gold," he called it, "when peace shall over all the earth / its ancient splendors fling, / and the whole world give back the song / which now the angels sing."

As the year leans again into Advent, why not allow for the coming of a Jesus beyond Jesus in the God of earth? Why not hope that the newborn God, incarnate as much of the nonhuman natural world around us as of a man from long ago, would be born also in us that through our relationship to the earth, to God, and to one another, we might set to rights the wrongs of an unsustainable world? Then from this blue-green sphere of home, as the carol tells, *earth* might sing back to *heaven* "glory" and "peace." Then, through love and joy, we might be saved.

Or maybe, situated here at the end of the year, with what is past and come what may, we are already saved. In relationship to the nonhuman natural world as Christ the incarnation of God, we are ever and always reconciled to heaven, reconciled to life.

If we would but believe.

These are the days when we begin to close up the Canadian cabin for winter. Dusk falls fast, and the lake is almost too cold for a swim. The sun's long gone when, bolstered by sauna heat, I muster the courage to dare a final dip. From the smooth stone shore, I dive. Chilly water steals my breath even as it buoys me up again, sputtering. A few strokes out, and I'm fine—cold, but all right. My body has adjusted. I'm just another animal under a soft autumn sky. I swim farther, and the ragged black line of treetops from the far shore offers up the moon, bleaching in its rise. Stroke, stroke, stroke, my chin in the water, my eyes above. I am small, virtually nothing in the world, yet swimming to the moon, its path comes straight to me. Try as I might to move without effect, my body and a light wind, too, ruffle the lake's surface. "Broken and broken," the poet Chosu wrote, "again on the sea, the moon / so easily mends."

If we would but believe.

Conclusion

"Holy persons draw to themselves all that is earthly."
—Hildegard of Bingen

How are we to be? I've lost it again, that shock of peace I mentioned stumbling over in the course of this experiment. I can't see past the trees of our yard—mere trees, the redwing blackbird nothing more than a bundle of blood and feathers and bone. How silly ever to imagine otherwise. There is nothing holy here. The nonhuman natural world is simply our environment, material stuff. It's fragile, and we're screwed.

I worry for the spotted fawn I saw by the edge of the reservoir, alone. There's a road, a new one, servicing a new subdivision. It passes much too close and the cars come much too fast for a doe preoccupied. I have to look away from those ridiculously large ears trained on me, away from the soft brown eyes and spindly legs.

Yard signs boasting "mosquito free" keep popping up around my neighborhood, and in my blooming garden, there are no butterflies. None. The EPA released its final report on fracking—surprise, it's really bad for water—but not before "approximately 6,800 sources of drinking water for public water systems were located within one mile of at least one hydraulically fractured well."[1] Those stats are for 2013. Where did my serenity go?

In the final paragraph of his famous essay, "Notes of a Native Son," James Baldwin writes,

> It began to seem that one would have to hold in the mind forever two ideas which seemed to be in opposition. The first idea was acceptance, the acceptance, totally without rancor, of life as it is, and men as they are: in the light of this idea, it goes without saying that injustice is a commonplace.

But this did not mean that one could be complacent, for the second idea was of equal power: that one must never, in one's own life, accept these injustices as commonplace but must fight them with all one's strength. This fight begins, however, in the heart and it now had been laid to my charge to keep my own heart free of hatred and despair. This intimation made my heart heavy.[2]

How are we to be? A heavy heart still beats. Come what may, the good news remains. "The Earth holds every possibility inside it," Kathleen Dean Moore observes, "and the mystery of transformation, one thing to another. This is the wildest comfort."[3]

As an experiment, that's how I've approached the question at the heart of this book. What happens if . . . ? Of the experiment, I say with no small degree of caution, that it seems to work—what Christians think of the traditional Jesus applies to the nonhuman natural world, too.

"Jesus" can include the earth itself.

So as it turns out, this experiment is also about the vocabulary of Christian theology—about forgiveness and salvation and sin and love. It is about the mystery of the man from Galilee that transcends time and place in the mythos of a religion, and in that transcendence pushes Jesus beyond Jesus. Definitions. What does it mean that . . . ? These are what drive the stuff of this book and continue to drive me on, hounded and haunted by the Christian tradition that I cannot seem to shake or leave behind.

From my days as an amateur scientist, I remember that any experiment worth the name must be replicable. You have to be able to undertake it again. Better yet, others, disinterested in its outcome, should run the trials, undertake the assays, carefully subject the question to test.

The year cycles round again and with it, an invitation to explore, to try again. As for me, I think I will. Then perhaps, by great grace and what faith I can muster, I'll get another glimpse. Maybe I'll find that equanimity, that peace.

As I paddle back, my eyes can't help but seek the shore where the fawn had watched me pass some minutes ago. Nothing. Then, when I'm almost past and feeling glum, out of the underbrush, a tawny doe steps. She wriggles her nose my way, and I watch the fawn bump her side. Exhale.

Notes

Introduction

1. Jane Goodall, "In the Forests of Gombe," in *The Best American Science and Nature Writing*, ed. Edward O. Wilson (New York: Houghton Mifflin, 2001), 51.

2. Wendell Berry, *A Continuous Harmony: Essays Cultural and Agricultural* (New York: Harcourt Brace Jovanovich, 1970), 6.

Part I

1. A quick caveat: of course earth already is, but in the Christian tradition, so is Jesus. The year is a cycle paradoxically tracing the temporal life of an eternal God. So just as traditional Christians anticipate in Advent (the eternal) Jesus's coming, so this experiment anticipates the coming God of earth—the earth returning—as an expression of the Christian Jesus.

Chapter 1: Heaven, All Bound Up with Earth

1. Gen. 2:1, 4.
2. Prov. 8:22–31; 3:19; 8:35–36.
3. John 1:1.

Chapter 2: Preparing, and the Terror of Uncertainty

1. "What Climate Change Means for Africa, Asia and the Coastal Poor," *The World Bank*, released June 19, 2013, http://www.worldbank.org/en/news/feature/2013/06/19/what-climate-change-means-africa-asia-coastal-poor (accessed March 10, 2015).

2. Matt. 3:1; cf. Isa. 40:3.

Chapter 3: Waiting, On Becoming Expert in Humility

1. Isa. 40:31.

Chapter 4: Anticipation

1. Rev. 1:13–15.
2. John 1:5.
3. Henry Beston, *The Outermost House* (New York: Doubleday, Doran and Co., 1928).

Part II: God, New-Born

1. John Muir, *The Writings of John Muir: My First Summer in the Sierra* (New York: Houghton Mifflin, 1917), 95.

Chapter 5: Our Awesome, Fragile World, Instructions Not Included

1. I'm grateful to Cliff Edwards for this.

Chapter 6: See Here, Wow

1. K. C. Cole, *Mind over Matter: Conversations with the Cosmos* (New York: Houghton Mifflin Harcourt, 2004), 111.
2. Pierre Teilhard de Chardin, *Writings in Time of War* (New York: Harper & Row, 1968), 124.
3. Annie Dillard, *Pilgrim at Tinker Creek* (New York: Harper & Row, 1974), 8.

Part III: The Glory of an Ordinary Earth

1. Though widely attributed to Einstein, I've been unable to find an original citation. The quote may derive from a remembered conversation with author David Reichenstien; see https://www.quora.com/What-quotes-are-most-commonly-misattributed-to-Albert-Einstein.

Chapter 7: Stories for Being

1. Jordan Kisner, "No Wonder It Quakes," in *The American Scholar*, Spring 2015, https://theamericanscholar.org/no-wonder-it-quakes/#.VYmB0KZi3Zs.
2. For details, see http://monarchwatch.org/bring-back-the-monarchs/campaign/the-details/.

Chapter 8: Locating Home

1. Robert Frost, "The Death of Hired Man," at *Poetry Foundation*, https://www.poetryfoundation.org/poems-and-poets/poems/detail /44261 (accessed May 26, 2015).
2. Wendell Berry, *A Continuous Harmony: Essays Cultural and Agricultural* (New York: Harcourt Brace Jovanovich, 1970), 52–53.
3. Barry Lopez, "Know Your Place with Barry Lopez," speech at Graham Oaks Nature Park, Wilsonville, Oregon, Sept. 21, 2011, https://www.youtube.com/watch?v=7TYjFrJ-02I (accessed Feb. 2015).
4. Variations of this phrase found in Matt. 3:17; Mark 1:11; and Luke 3:22; see also John 1:32–34.

Chapter 9: Friendship and All the Stuff of Earth

1. Jan Rocha and Jonathan Watts, "Brazil Salutes Chico Mendes 25 Years after His Murder," *The Guardian* (December 20, 2013), http://www.theguardian.com/world/2013/dec/20/brazil-salutes-chico -mendes-25-years-after-murder (accessed April 20, 2015).
2. Matt. 26:11 (my trans.).
3. Variations of this story told in Matt. 19:16–22; Mark 10:17–27; and Luke 18:18–23.

Chapter 10: Dust, or When Holiness Wears Thin

1. Gen. 4:14 (my trans.).
2. Gen. 3:19 (my trans.).
3. Job 38:4.
4. Job 42:6.

Chapter 11: Hunger

1. Robert Farrar Capon, *The Supper of the Lamb: A Culinary Reflection* (New York: Modern Library, 2002), 115.
2. See Isa. 58:5–7.

Chapter 12: At Earth's Table

1. Carl Sagan, *Cosmos* (New York: Random House, 1980), 218.
2. See 1 Cor. 11:17–34.
3. Pablo Neruda, "The Great Tablecloth," in *Extravagaria*, trans. Alastair Reid (New York: Farrar, Straus and Giroux, 2001).

4. Annie Dillard, *Pilgrim at Tinker Creek* (New York: Harper & Row, 1974), 242.

5. Peter Mayer, "Bountiful" in *Bountiful* (Stillwater, MN: Blue Boat, 1998).

Chapter 13: Principalities, Passion, and Power

1. See https://www.350.org.

2. Bill McKibben, "Copenhagen: Things Fall Apart and an Uncertain Future Looms," *Yale Environment 360* (blog), December 21, 2009, http://e360.yale.edu/feature/copenhagen_things_fall_apart_and_an_uncertain_future_looms/2225 (accessed February 2015).

Chapter 14: Grief

1. Kathleen Dean Moore, "Red Sky at Morning: Ethics and the Oceanic Crisis," speech at Gustavus Adolphus College, Oct. 3, 2012, https://www.youtube.com/watch?v=K3GpQu0IpmM (accessed April 3, 2015).

2. Ibid.

Chapter 15: Was There Compost in the Garden of Eden?

1. Ecumenical Patriarch Bartholomew, "Exclusive: Patriarch Bartholomew on Pope Francis' Climate Encyclical," *Time* (June 18, 2015) http://time.com/3926076/pope-francis-encyclical-patriarch-bartholomew/ (accessed June 20, 2015).

Chapter 16: The Comedy of Surprise

1. Eric Wallace, "Eco Punks," in *Blue Ridge Outdoors* (May, 2015): 15–16.

2. Ibid.

3. Charles Wright, *Littlefoot*, stanza 6, in *Bye-and-Bye: Selected Late Poems* (New York: Farrar, Straus, and Giroux, 2011), 216.

4. John 20:29.

5. Terry Tempest Williams, *An Unspoken Hunger: Stories from the Field* (New York: Vintage, 1994), 86-87.

6. e. e. cummings, "i thank you God for most this amazing day," https://www.poetryfoundation.org/features/audio/detail/76999 (accessed May 26, 2016).

Chapter 17: Now, Go; and Be Here

1. Chase Twichell, "Vestibule" in *Horses Where the Answers Should Have Been: New and Selected Poems* (Seattle: Copper Canyon Press, 2013).

2. See http://www.juliabutterfly.com/-julia.html.

3. Barbara Kingsolver, *Small Wonder* (New York: Harper Collins, 2002) 108.

4. Quoted by Terry Tempest Williams, *An Unspoken Hunger*, 89.

5. Carson's oft-quoted observation first appeared in "Help Your Child to Wonder" in *Woman's Home Companion* (July, 1956), 25–27, 46-48 and later in *The Sense of Wonder* (New York: Harper, 1965).

6. Terry Tempest Williams, *An Unspoken Hunger*, 130, 131.

Chapter 18: Wonder and Works, or a Gardener's Peculiar Constitution

1. Check it out in Rom. 3:28.

2. Bill McKibben, "Eaarth; Making a Life on a Tough new Planet," speech at Dominican University of California, April 28, 2010, https://www.youtube.com/watch?v=rQ3PTDLadTo (accessed April 2015).

3. Ibid.

4. Quoted in T. C. McLuhan, *The Way of the Earth* (New York: Simon and Schuster, 1995), 150.

Chapter 19: Judgment and Mercy

1. Wendell Berry, *Home Economics* (San Francisco: North Point Press, 1987), 139.

2. Matt. 5:17.

3. Rom. 2:5–11.

4. Rev. 19:11–16.

5. Wendell Berry, *Home Economics* (San Francisco: North Point Press, 1987), 139.

Chapter 20: With Wild Delight, a Mandate for Joy

1. Barry Lopez, "Sliver of Sky" in *Harper's* (January 2013) http://harpers.org/archive/2013/01/sliver-of-sky/ (accessed February 10, 2015).

2. Dacher Keltner, co-author, reporting in *Science Daily* as quoted in *The Week*, Feb. 20, 2015, 21.

3. Elizabeth Barrett Browning, "Aurora Leigh" A Poem" (1864) http://digital.library.upenn.edu/women/barrett/aurora/aurora.html (accessed March 10, 2015).

4. George Washington Carver, http://www.africanamericanquotes.org /george-washington-carver.html (accessed January 21, 2015).

5. Fra Giovanni, *A Letter to the Most Illustrious the Contessina Allagia Dela Aldobrandeschi, Written Christmas Eve Anno Domini 1513*, in *Respectfully Quoted: A Dictionary of Quotations* by James H. Billington (Library of Congress: Courier Corporation, 2010), 274–75.

6. Isa. 65:17.

Conclusion

1. Executive Summary, "Hydraulic Fracturing Drinking Water Assessment," http://www2.epa.gov/hfstudy (accessed June 2015).

2. James Baldwin, *Notes of a Native Son* (1955; repr., Boston: Beacon Press, 1984), 113–14.

3. Kathleen Dean Moore, "Wild Comfort," blog on *Wild Comfort: The Solace of Nature* (Boston: Trumpeter, 2010), http://www.riverwalking .com/wild-comfort.html.

50376689R00097

Made in the USA
Middletown, DE
30 October 2017